LEADER'S GUIDE

LIFE in the SPIRIT

YOUTH EDITION

ROBERTSON MCQUILKIN

LifeWay Press
Nashville, Tennessee

ISBN: 0-7673-2595-8

Dewey Decimal Classification: 231.3
Subject Heading: SPIRITUAL LIFE \ HOLY SPIRIT

This book is the text for course CG-0379 in the subject area "Personal Life" of the Christian Growth Study Plan.

Printed in the United States of America

LifeWay Press
127 Ninth Avenue, North
Nashville, Tennessee 37234-0151

[CONTENTS]

[THE AUTHOR]

Robertson McQuilkin

Robertson McQuilkin is a homemaker, conference speaker, and writer.

Robertson served as president of Columbia International University, Columbia, South Carolina, for 22 years. In 1990 he stepped down to care full time for his wife Muriel, who had reached the stage of Alzheimer's disease in which she needed the care of her husband 24 hours a day. To his surprise, that decision which he considered easy and unremarkable continues to echo throughout the evangelical world. Two articles about Muriel, "Living Vows" and "Muriel's Blessing," have been published in dozens of magazines and books in many languages.

Robertson and Muriel served in full partnership as missionaries in Japan for 12 years prior to his presidency at Columbia. In Columbia, Muriel started many ministries: a TV puppet show for children, a morning radio talk show, ministries among students' wives, along with constant counseling, entertaining, and various art projects.

The McQuilkins have six children. Mardi is an artist, living with her husband in Myrtle Beach, South Carolina; Bob is in heaven, having died in a diving accident in 1988; David is an executive with Xerox in Japan and the father of two; Jan is a pastor's wife in Wisconsin and mother of three; Amy serves with her husband as missionaries to Japan and has three children; Kent ministers among the slum dwellers of Calcutta, India.

Robertson has written scores of articles for journals or as chapters in books and has published several books, three of which continue to have wide influence: *An Introduction to Biblical Ethics, The Great Omission,* and *Understanding and Applying the Bible.*

[LEADING THIS STUDY]

Note: Page numbers identified in this *Leader's Guide* will be designated "LG."
All other page references refer to pages in the member book.

Thank you for choosing to facilitate a study of *Life in the Spirit, Youth Edition.* Whether you're coordinating multiple groups in your church or leading a small group in your home, I hope you will find this *Leader's Guide* helpful and meaningful to your preparation each week. The more familiar you are with the message and the resources of *Life in the Spirit,* the better prepared you will be to lead your group. Complete the following activities to familiarize yourself with this course. Check off each action that you complete.

In *Life in the Spirit, Youth Edition* Member Book:

- ❑ Read the Foreword (p. 5) and day 1 of week 1 (pp. 7-9).
- ❑ Examine the course map on the inside front cover.
- ❑ Read the Table of Contents (p. 3) to get an overall view of the course.

In this Leader Guide (LG):

- ❑ Read the Table of Contents and scan through this *Leader's Guide* to familiarize yourself with the learning aids. Notice that most weeks involve handouts and group session activities.
- ❑ Read the remainder of this section and decide how you'll conduct the study.

Decide when and where groups will meet. We recommend one- to two-hour small-group sessions. One hour is a minimum. Groups should allow two hours if they intend to deal fully with the material covered.

When you have determined the duration of the study, consult the church calendar to find a time for 12 to 24 consecutive weeks with very few interruptions. This will help members continue the habit of completing their daily study and, most importantly, spending time with God. If after four or five weeks members have more than one week off, they tend to lose the momentum, and resuming the study is that much more difficult.

Groups may meet at the church, in homes, or other locations convenient to youth. You may want to offer group studies at a variety of times and locations so more youth will be able to participate. Consider these options:

Sunday evenings

- Meet before or after evening worship.

Weekdays

- Meet at the church at a convenient time to those involved.
- Meet in members' homes. Be sure to set guidelines about group dismissal, so the group does not wear out its welcome.

Decide on the number of groups needed. Work with your youth pastor, youth leaders, discipleship director, minister of education, or other church leaders to determine how many youth in your church want to study this course at this time. Publicize the study in your church newspaper or bulletin, your youth newsletters, and on posters placed in the youth area of the church. Remember that you will need one group for every 10 members.

Enlist leaders. Each group will need a separate leader. Youth Minister, you may want to lead the first group and train 8 to 10 persons to provide leadership for future groups. If you need more leaders, you may want to take 2 or more groups through the study at different times during the week. Leading the first group will demonstrate your belief in what *Life in the Spirit* is about. It also will be enriching and helpful in your walk with the Lord. If you are unable to lead the first group, enlist another church staff member or lay leader.

Pray that God will help you identify those persons He wants to lead the groups. These leaders should be spiritually growing Christians and active church members. Leaders should have teachable spirits, the ability to relate well to youth, a commitment to keep information private, and a willingness to spend the time necessary to prepare for the sessions. Also, look for people who possess skills for leading small-group learning activities. Do not select someone who is having spiritual, marital, or physical difficulties that could hinder their effectiveness.

Promote the study. Use the promotion master on LG p. 41 in church newsletters, as a bulletin insert, or enlarge it and use it as a poster.

Enlist participants. Invite church leaders and other prospective participants to the introductory session (LG p. 13). This session will provide enough information for them to decide whether to participate in the study. At the end of the session, give those present an opportunity to sign up for the course. If persons are unwilling to make the necessary commitment to the individual and group study, ask them not to participate at this time.

Use the same criteria for all leaders. If you don't have qualified leaders, start a waiting list and encourage members to pray that God will call out additional leaders. Some leaders might be willing to lead a second group at a different time during the week since little additional preparation would be required.

Order resources. Order resources 8 to 10 weeks prior to the introductory session. Although your order will arrive only a week or two after your order, leaders need time to prepare for the overview session and time to enlist participants. Order 8 to 10 member books and one leader guide for each leader. Resources include:

Life in the Spirit, Member Book (0-7673-2594-X)
Life in the Spirit, Leader Guide (0-7673-2595-8)

Prepare or secure additional resources. Much of your course preparation can be completed at one time. If you will complete the following actions, you will save time for personal and spiritual preparation during the course.

1. Make one copy of the following pages in this Leader Guide for each member. If possible, use heavier card stock for the Scripture Memory Cards or paste them on card stock after copying.
- Group-session Handouts (LG p. 45-61)
- Scripture Memory Cards (LG p. 39)
- Keeping a Spiritual Journal (LG p. 38)
- Leader Evaluation Form (LG p. 40)
- Group Covenant (LG p. 62)

2. Prepare the following posters:
- Memorizing Scripture poster—Turn to "Help Members Memorize Scripture" (LG p. 10-11). Write the boldface instructions or key words on a poster for use in the introductory and first small-group sessions.
- *Life in the Spirit* course map (inside front cover of the members book).

3. Provide chalkboard, overhead projector, or flipchart for use throughout the course. They will be needed on several occasions. Extra sheets of paper will be required in several sessions. Keep a supply in your room.

Optional videos. The adult study of *Life in the Spirit* included using two optional videos. You may want to use segments from these videos with your youth *Life in the Spirit* study.

Select a theme song. Youth learn much of their theology through music. Music is a valuable way to stimulate a spiritual and emotional response to the topics being studied. Consider selecting and singing (or playing a recorded version) of a theme song for this study. Using a hymnal or songbook is always best because the leader does not have to be concerned about infringing the copyright law. If you must duplicate a song, make sure that the selection chosen is not copyrighted, or if it is, that you have secured the proper permission to duplicate it.

Set and collect fees. We recommend that participants pay at least part of the cost of the materials so they make a commitment to the study with a financial investment. Announce the fee when you enlist participants so they will not be caught off guard or embarrassed at the introductory session. You may want to provide scholarships for those unable to participate due to lack of financial resources.

Keep records. A Christian Growth Study Plan diploma may be awarded to a member who completes *Life in the Spirit.* Instructions appear on page 160 (LG p. 63). Plan to award diplomas during a worship service or at another appropriate time when the church family can affirm participants. Diplomas recognize the significant work of the participants.

How to Use This Guide for a Small-Group Study

This *Leader's Guide* assists you in preparing for and conducting the small-group learning sessions for a study of *Life in the Spirit, Youth Edition.* Pages 11-37 of this guide provide step-by-step procedures for conducting an introductory session and 12 group sessions. Each of the group sessions includes three parts:

- *Before the Session*—This section includes actions for you to complete prior to the group session. On LG page 43 you will find a standard Before the Session list that will be referenced but not repeated each session. You may want to cut out this half page of your book and use it as a bookmark for this guide. The back side contains the standard After the Session list.

- *During the Session*—This section provides activities for you to use in conducting a one- to two-hour small-group session. You will find that the activities suggested will require more than one hour to process effectively. Don't get frustrated if you are limited to one-hour sessions. Adapt the activities and use the ones that are most helpful. The activities for the session follow a similar pattern each week. This simplifies your leadership role, but you should feel free to rearrange or adapt the sessions according to your group's needs.

- *After the Session*—This section guides you in evaluating the group session, your performance as a leader, and the needs of group members. This will help you improve your group leadership skills. As mentioned earlier, a standard After the Session list is on LG page 44. Cut it out and use it as a bookmark for quick reference at the end of each session. You'll want to record in your journal answers to the questions contained in the standard After the Session list.

The group sessions require a minimum of leader preparation so you can give yourself to prayer and personal spiritual preparation. If you adapt the lesson plans or create activities of your own, remember to secure any resources that are required for these activities.

Each week you are encouraged to think about your group members and identify one or more who may need a personal contact from you. Do not neglect this aspect of your ministry. Your primary assignment in this study is to help youth develop Spirit-filled living, not just teach knowledge about the Spirit.

Objectives of the Small-Group Sessions

The purpose of the small-group meeting is to express and process what each member has been studying during the preceding week. Each session will have two objectives: understanding and experience. To help group members understand the material, you will lead the group in activities such as reviewing and interacting. To help them to experience *Life in the Spirit, Youth Edition*, you will lead the group in activities like testimony, prayer, and singing.

Understanding begins with knowing the key points of the unit. To be sure all members understand, self-evaluation exercises will help, but we must move beyond ability to recall the facts. To help each member understand the meaning and the implications of the teaching, you will lead in interaction as a group.

The goal of this course, however, is not to gain information but to personally experience life in the Spirit. To gauge spiritual growth is much more difficult than measuring knowledge and understanding. You can help your youth move beyond the elementary stages of learning.

I want to encourage you to devote a major part of the group time to experiencing life in the Spirit. You will facilitate group members experience by:

- *Singing*—Each week I've suggested ways to worship and fellowship with the Spirit through song. You do not have to be a musician to sing together in the group. Prepare needed music ahead of time. If necessary, enlist someone to lead the group to sing.

- *Personal sharing*—Both telling the story of the Spirit's activity and the hearing of it help us experience His work in our lives.

- *Self-evaluation*—Honesty about our struggles is not easy, nor is evaluating the other members of the group. But we can help one another along the upward spiral.

- *Encourage obedience*—Feelings about the Spirit are of no value if we don't actually connect with Him. Connection comes when we activate the will. Choosing to obey the truths we have studied is the connection.

- *Praying together*—We express our choices in prayer. So prayer—in pairs, in quads, and in the entire group—is a critical part of our group experience.

As you lead your group, concentrate on the five elements above. In these ways we help one another experience victory over temptation, growth toward likeness to Jesus, and, best of all, companionship with God.

Role of the Small-Group Leader

You may feel inadequate in leading a study about *Life in the Spirit*. You may not think you are knowledgeable enough. Such thoughts and feelings are OK. Your role in this small-group study is not that of a teacher. You are a facilitator of a group-learning process. You will be helping members help each other by applying *Hebrews 10:24* (NASB), *Let us consider how to stimulate one another to love and good deeds.*

If God has led you to accept this assignment, you can trust Him to equip and enable you to accomplish the task. You are an instrument through which God wants to do His work. Without God you can do nothing of Kingdom value. With Him you can move spiritual mountains. Depend on God and *pray continually (1 Thess. 5:17)*. Keep in mind that the Holy Spirit is present in every session to work in and through you. You are not guiding this group alone!

Group members will be spending time daily studying *Life in the Spirit, Youth Edition*. The Holy Spirit will serve as their Teacher, for no spiritual truth can be understood without His involvement. The content and learning activities will help youth learn the basic truths and principles during the week.

Members will be working on application of the truths even before coming to the group time. Your role is to help each youth understand and experience the truths of the unit just completed.

Much of the understanding and application will happen in the group session each week. This *Leader's Guide* will provide the resources you need to lead effectively, but don't limit yourself to the group session.

Think of each member as a personal prayer responsibility. Try to discern the spiritual health and responses of each youth and bring those to the Lord daily in your private prayer. The Spirit may give you a nudge to reach out personally to some member outside of class time by a telephone call, letter, or lunch or soda together. Like a shepherd with his sheep, God may give you the high privilege of helping some of your members find the path to *green pastures* and *quiet waters* until the Holy Spirit restores their souls and keeps them on *paths of righteousness (Ps. 23).*

You should expect that youth will ask some questions you cannot answer. What you do in response will help them learn to turn to the Lord, His Word, and other believers for assistance. When you do not have an answer (or perhaps even when you do), encourage the group to join you in praying and searching the Scriptures together for an answer. A question may become an extra homework assignment for members to study during the week. Together, ask God to guide you to His answer, to His perspective. Then trust God to do it. When God sends the answer through one or more people in the group, you and your members will come to trust Him more.

Grouping Members During the Session

In During the Session, each activity has a recommended grouping. The size of the sub-groups is based on the content to be shared and the amount of time available. If you decide to make grouping changes, evaluate what youth will be sharing, how much time you have, and what group size would provide for maximum participation. The following descriptions explain the terms used in this guide.

- *Small Group*—Refers to a group of 6 to 10 persons including the small-group leader. Unless a different group size is suggested, the activities during the session are for use with the entire small group.

- *Quads*—Refers to four people. Depending on the size of your group, each quad actually may have 3, 4, or 5 members. For instance, if you have 10 members we recommend 2 quads of 3 members and 1 quad with 4. You could, however, have 2 groups of 5. When you divide into quads, verbally give the assignment to all members. You may need to assign 1 member in each quad as the leader.

- *Pairs*—Refers to two people. If you have an odd number of people, one pair will need to have three members, or the extra person could work with you to form a pair.

Include yourself as you can in these small groupings for sharing and discussion. You will not only model a participating attitude, but you will also have the opportunity to share and grow with the group. They need to see you doing the same things you are asking them to do.

Getting Started

Develop a Time Schedule. Each group session is designed with these four segments:

- Knowing
- Understanding
- Experiencing
- Responding

I have sometimes included an arrival activity in addition to the four segments. Usually the Knowing segment will constitute an arrival activity.

You'll find time recommendations beside each segment. For example, a typical unit may contain a schedule such as:

1. Arrival Activity (10 min.)
2. Knowing (40 min.)
3. Understanding (20 min.)
4. Experiencing (25 min.)
5. Responding (25 min.)

Each session is planned for two hours. If you do not have two hours in your meeting schedule, you may use one of four optional approaches.

1. Shorten the recommended times of each segment of the session to fit a one- or one-and-one-half-hour format.

2. Divide the sessions into two meetings per week. For example, you might meet for one hour on Sunday and a second hour on Wednesday.

3. Take two weeks per unit of study. Complete individual study and use the first hour's agenda for the first group session. Encourage individual review of the unit during the second week and use the second hour's agenda for the second group session. This option requires a minimum of 25 weeks—an introductory session and 24 group sessions.

4. Rethink the time schedule to provide for the two-hour format.

Obviously you must tailor the schedule to your youth, your situation, and your ministry area. Use your discretion in planning times, but do not shorten the session so much that the group is rushed. A *Life in the Spirit* group needs to be experiential. The youth must have some time to focus on their response to the Spirit.

Encourage members to keep a spiritual journal. Participants will need to keep a spiritual journal during the course, and hopefully will continue to long after the course is completed. This journal will be organized during the introductory session or at least by the first group session. Here are several suggestions:

- Three-ring binder with notebook paper and tabs.
- Spiral-bound notebook, preferably with section dividers included.
- Bound "diary" type book with blank pages.
- *DiscipleHelps: A Daily Quiet Time Guide and Journal* includes a prayer focus for each day, Bible study Worksheets, Scripture Memory verses, a Bible reading plan, plus tips on jotting down each day's thoughts. You can obtain *DiscipleHelps: A Daily Quiet Time Guide and Journal* (item 0805494511) from the Customer Service Center; 127 Ninth Avenue, North; Nashville, TN 37234; 1-800-458-2772; or from Baptist Book Stores and LifeWay Christian Stores.

You may want to provide the same kind of notebook for each member. If so, secure one for each member before the first session and include the cost in the fee for the class. Whether you provide the notebooks or allow members to select their own, provide each member with a copy of Keeping a Spiritual Journal, LG page 38.

Help members memorize Scripture. Some of your group members may not be skilled at memorizing Scripture. The following suggestions may be helpful. Write the boldface instructions on a poster for use in the introductory and first small-group session. Be prepared to explain each of the suggestions.

1. Write the verse and reference on an index card.

2. Seek understanding. Read the verse in its context. For example, if you are memorizing *2 Corinthians 3:18* you may want to read *2 Corinthians 3:7-18.* Study the verse and try to understand its meaning.

3. Read the verse aloud several times.

4. Learn to quote the verse one phrase at a time. Divide the verse into short and meaningful phrases. Learn to quote the first phrase word for word. Then build on it by learning the second phrase. Continue until you are able to quote the entire verse word for word.

5. Repeat the verse to another person and ask him to check your accuracy.

6. Review the memorized verse regularly. During the first week, carry the card in your pocket or purse. Pull it out for review several times daily during waiting periods—like riding to school or work, taking a coffee or lunch break. Review the verse at least daily for the first six weeks. Review weekly for the next six weeks and monthly thereafter.

Model Openness by Seeking Evaluation.
In the latter portion of *Life in the Spirit* youth will deal with developing their spiritual gifts by seeking evaluation from others. You can both improve your skills and model such openness for the group by seeking the group's evaluation of your leadership. Use the Leader Evaluation form on LG page 40.

Be Flexible!
I've outlined in some detail guidelines for leading your small group. To follow this pattern is better than free-lancing each session. But sometimes exceptions arise. Stay alert for times you need to change the schedule.

For example, you may realize that most of the group has missed a major teaching of the unit. Don't move on. Instead, stretch the allotted time and cut back on some other segment of the session. On the other hand, some member simply may not "get it" no matter how long you spend on the subject. Others may have a hobby horse they want to ride and eat up precious time allotted for other important activities. In such cases, suggest that you get together after the session for further interaction. Remember that our objective is not to settle every doctrinal detail but to experience the fullness of life in the Spirit.

Remember, as we study the work of the Holy Spirit in our lives and seek to connect with His light and power, He just might want to break loose among us! I've been in meetings where the program was set and part of it was to be a time of sharing testimonies. But suddenly something unexpected happened. Instead of a traditional testimony of God's blessing, someone spoke who either had or wanted a powerful encounter with God.

Look for the signs of the Holy Spirit moving through your group. I always face a dilemma as the leader to know whether to set aside the scheduled program or to decide the time has come to pull things back into the order planned. If the Spirit wants to do a special work in your group, He can and will enable you to respond appropriately. I have learned, however, that you must make some prior commitments in the the way you function as a spiritual leader. You must give your plans and agenda to God ahead of time. If He interrupts your group, cancel your agenda and see what the Spirit has in mind.

Here are some suggestions for responding to the Spirit's activity in your group:

1. Watch for things like tears of joy or conviction, emotional or spiritual brokenness, the thrill of a newfound insight, or an opportunity for prayer in response to a need. These things are sometimes seen only as a facial expression. Determine whether you need to talk to the person now with the group or privately. You must depend on the Holy Spirit for such guidance.

2. Respond by asking a probing question such as:
   - *Is something happening in your life right now that you would share with us?*
   - *How can we pray for you?*
   - *Would you share with us what God is doing in your life?*
   - *What can we do to be of help to you?*

3. If someone responds by sharing, then provide ministry based on the need. If the youth does not seem ready to respond, do not push or pressure. Give God time to work in his or her life.

4. Invite youth to share in ministry to each other. This may be to pray, to comfort, to counsel privately, or to rejoice with the person. When you do not feel equipped to deal with a problem that surfaces, ask the group if one of them feels led to help. You will be amazed at how God works to provide just the right person to minister to a need.

5. Give youth the opportunity to testify to what God is doing. This is a very critical point. Often the testimony of one youth may be used of God to help another youth with an identical problem or challenge. This is also one of the best ways for youth to experience God by hearing testimony of His wonderful work in the life of another person. Do not hide God's glory from His people.

6. When you don't sense a clear direction about what to do next, ask the group. You might ask, "Does anyone have a sense of what God would want us to do?" Often God will guide through one of the other members or through a group consensus.

I cannot explain all that you may need to do. I cannot give you directions for handling every situation. But I can speak from experience: If God wants to work in the midst of a group, He can and will give the guidance needed for that time. Your job is to learn to know His voice and then do everything you sense He wants you to do. At the same time trust Him to work through His body—the church. He has placed members in your group and gifted them to build up the body of Christ. Acknowledge and use all of the resources God has given to your group.

INTRODUCTION

Introductory Goals

Potential youth members will:
- overview the content of the course
- discover how the course is designed to help them experience life in the Spirit
- understand what will be expected of them in this course
- demonstrate a commitment to complete the individual study and group session requirements for the course.

Before the Session

- ❑ Prepare yourself spiritually through prayer for the upcoming session. Ask the Spirit to draw people to the introductory session that He wants to involve in this study.
- ❑ Read through "During the Session." Adapt or develop the activities in a way that will best help your group understand the overview of the content and make a commitment to participate.
- ❑ Decide on the amount of time to allow for each activity. Plan for one hour. Subsequent sessions are designed for two hours. If you have less than two hours for group sessions you will need to adapt the recommended times for the length of your sessions. Write a time in the margin to indicate when each activity should begin.
- ❑ Have on hand copies of the member's book for each anticipated participant.
- ❑ Make arrangements to have an overhead projector.
- ❑ Prepare an overhead cel or poster of the suggestions for memorizing Scripture.
- ❑ Secure the theme hymn or chorus for each person.
- ❑ Be prepared to register those who decide to participate in the course. If members will pay for their own books, decide how you will collect book fees. You may want to enlist a person to receive the fees after the session.
- ❑ If you have not read and completed all the preparations in "Leading a Small-group Study of *Life in the Spirit*," do so before the introductory session.

During the Session

Arrival Activity (10 min.)

1. Greet prospective members as they arrive. Give a copy of *Life in the Spirit* member book to each attendee. Divide the group into pairs. Ask each pair to examine the contents page as an introduction to the sessions that are designed to launch them into a new dimension of life in the Spirit. Suggest they share with each other lessons that particularly intrigue them or raise questions.
2. After pairs have had sufficient time to look through the book, offer an opening prayer. Pray that God will use this session to give insight into how members can develop a life lived in the power and presence of the Holy Spirit. Ask God to guide each person in making a decision about whether or not to study *Life in the Spirit*.
3. Share with the group your reasons for a commitment to study *Life in the Spirit* and let them feel your enthusiasm for what lies ahead.
4. Sing together the hymn or chorus you have chosen as a theme for the course.

Course Overview (20 min.)

1. Explain that this study is not intended to be a gimmick, a technique, or 10 easy steps to experience life in the Spirit. Rather, the personal workbook and the small-group sessions are designed to help youth develop a relationship with the Holy Spirit that will produce greater likeness to Jesus.
2. Refer to the contents page and give a one-sentence explanation or "teaser" of the content for each session.
3. Call attention to the course map on the inside front cover of the member book. Briefly review the map to help participants visualize the connection between the activities of the Spirit. Refer to unit 1 for an explanation of the course map, but do not try to fully explain the map at this point.
4. Review the course requirements. Explain how this course offers a personal, in-depth approach to developing life in the Spirit. Explain the requirements of self- study and participation in the small-group sessions. Emphasize that participants will need to set aside 30 minutes a day five days a week to complete assignments. Suggest that members who are not able to commit their time to the individual and small-group study should not participate at this time. Offer to put names on a list for announcements of future studies when schedules may be more conducive to participation.
3. Announce when and where groups will be meeting to study *Life in the Spirit*.
4. Call for and answer any questions participants may have regarding the content of the course or course requirements.

Getting Ready for Next Week (20 min.)

Ask the group to open their Member Books to page

7. Using the following outline, describe the process for self-study that members will use during the coming week prior to the first small-group session.

1. *Unit Page.* Describe the various elements of the unit page. Point out the memory verse on the unit page. Using the Scripture memory overhead cel or poster, suggest ways members can memorize Scripture.
2. *Daily Assignments.* Explain how content is divided into five daily assignments. Encourage members to study only one day at a time, so they will have time to think about and apply the teachings in their lives. Explain that if they decide to participate in the study, their first assignment will be to complete the daily work for unit 1 before the first small-group meeting.
3. *Learning Activities.* Point out one of the learning activities with the symbol and indented type. Encourage members to complete all learning activities. Some will be simple, others more difficult; but working through each activity will be essential to fully understand the meaning and implications of the content. Optional: Consider doing one of the learning activities together.
4. *Spiritual Journal.* Turn to page 24 in the member book and read the section on spiritual journaling. Encourage keeping a journal, at least for the duration of the course. Perhaps, it will become a lifelong habit!
5. *Prayer. Life in the Spirit* centers around listening and talking with God and so must this course of study.

- Before each daily lesson. Encourage beginning each lesson by asking the Lord to be your teacher and making yourself fully available to Him. "Speak, Lord, your servant is listening."
- At the end of lessons. Turn to page 9 (the end of day 1) and point out the sample prayer. Explain that members should always end their day's study with prayer. Many lessons provide instructions for or examples of prayer. Members may use sample prayers as their own or simply as a suggestion for their personal approach to God. Say: **Turn to page 12 (the end of day 2) and note that the author may not write a prayer but simply suggest something you may wish to talk with God about. The most important part of the lesson may be concluding it with prayer—bringing closure to all the Spirit has been talking to you about.**
- Prayer partners. Suggest that every member enlist a person to be a prayer partner with him or her during this study. This person could be a group member, family member, or a close friend. Ask members to share regularly with this person specific ways they can pray for him or her as they grow in living life in the Spirit.

Decision Time/Closing (10 min.)

1. *Registration, Books, and Fees.* Describe the process for members to register for the course. Announce the book fee and tell members how to pay the fee.
2. Ask members to turn to page 6 in the member book and read aloud the covenant agreement. If you have made a cel or poster of the Group Covenant on LG page 62, use it at this time. Give members an opportunity to discuss any changes or additions they want to make. Seek full agreement on the covenant. Then ask members to make the changes agreed to on their copies. Ask them to fill in their name at the top.
3. Ask those who are willing to make a commitment to the course to sign their own covenant.
4. Call for a time of silent prayer. Ask those present to pray about their participation in *Life in the Spirit.* After a period of time, lead a prayer requesting God's guidance about the decisions being made and for blessing on the coming weeks of study.

After the Session

- ❑ In your personal list of those enrolled in your small group, make a note of any facts or impressions you have gleaned that will help you in your daily prayer for each member.
- ❑ Read and complete the evaluations and activities described in the Standard After the Session instructions (LG p. 44).
- ❑ Save all overhead cels for use in later sessions.
- ❑ Give the information from the registration sheets to the appropriate person in your church (if your small group is church-sponsored). If you have more than 10 people per group, enlist additional leaders for every 8 to 10 people prior to the first small-group session.
- ❑ Secure additional resources as needed. If you don't have enough member books, call 1-800-458-2772 to place an order or check with your local Baptist Book Store or LifeWay Christian Store for copies.

THE SPIRIT, THE SPIRAL

Session 1 Goals

Youth will:

- get acquainted with other members of the small group
- understand the flow of the course.

Before the Session

- ❑ Refer to standard Before the Session procedures.
- ❑ Arrange chairs in groupings of four.
- ❑ Gather the following items and include any others you need for activities you may have developed on your own:
- extra copies of the member's book for any new members
- arrange for any new members to have an orientation sometime following the group session
- paper and pencils
- a copy of the Get Acquainted questions (handout 1a) (LG p. 45) for each member
- a copy of the Unit 1 Review Quiz (handout 1b) for each member (LG p. 46)
- optional overhead cel or poster of the unit 1 questions
- the overhead cel or poster on memorizing Scripture used in the introductory session.

During the Session

Most of the activities for this session will be accomplished in small groups of four called quads. You may need to have three or five members in some groups if your enrollment is an uneven number. Remember, each time you divide the small group into pairs or quads, give verbal instructions to everyone. You may want to write the instructions on a chalkboard or newsprint. Members should stay in the same seating arrangement throughout the session. After a small-group experience, simply ask the group to direct their attention toward you without completely rearranging the chairs.

The activities of every small group session will follow this sequence:

1. Knowing
2. Understanding
3. Experiencing
4. Responding

- *Knowing* will include activities that review the contents of the unit such as a quiz, group review, and quoting the memory verse in pairs.
- *Understanding* will involve activities such as soliciting questions that are still unresolved and interaction in quads or as a whole group.
- *Experiencing* will contain activities such as sharing testimonies, personal application, and singing.
- *Responding* will involve prayer—individual, by pairs or quads, and in the group as a whole. This is the time when you will seek to lead youth to make some specific commitments concerning the teaching of the unit.

Arrival Activity (15 min.)

1. Greet members as they arrive and give each member a copy of the Get Acquainted statements (handout 1a). Seat them in groupings of four. While others are coming in, ask members to complete the statements in the handout.
2. Ask the quads to share with each other their responses to *a, d,* and *e*. Reconvene the large group and ask volunteers to share responses to *a, f,* and *g*. Collect the papers so you will have names, addresses, and phone numbers.
3. Lead an opening prayer. Thank God for bringing this group of youth together. Acknowledge God's presence in your midst and ask the Holy Spirit to be your Teacher during the session. Ask Him to begin bonding your lives together in Christian love and unity during the sessions of this study.

Knowing (25 min.)

1. *Content Review.* Ask the quads that are seated together to choose a presider and a recorder. Distribute the Unit 1 Review Quiz (handout 1b). Each quad should interact briefly, coming to a consensus on an answer to each question. Explain that the purpose here is to review what was presented in the unit, not to start from scratch and theorize on other possibilities. The recorder should note the consensus answers for later sharing with the entire group.
2. Reconvene the large group and ask for answers to each question, noting them on the chalkboard or overhead transparency. Each member should fill in any answers missing from his or her review list for later use. For a full answer, refer back to the lesson under review. Here are possible short answers to put on the unit outline on chalkboard, or overhead transparency. Don't provide the answers in advance; try to draw answers from the members. Synonyms are acceptable answers.

1. God. Members may have put Jesus or the Bible, though they really should put "God as revealed in the Bible" if they choose the Bible as the answer.

2. A new creation and a new relationship. *Regeneration* or *indwelling* would be technical terms someone may suggest.
3. I must know, surrender, and trust—know certain basic facts, surrender my will unconditionally to God, and trust the Holy Spirit to keep His promise and bring me to His goal for me.
4. • We become more like Jesus.
   • We get closer to Him in daily companionship.
   • We get a greater love relationship with God.
5. Gifts and witness for sure, but the full answer would also include evangelism and world missions. Spirit-given abilities are varied; but all are for serving God through His church, thus serving people.

This review serves the purpose of knowing what was covered, not for settling all problems. Explain that the group will return to these issues for interaction at a later time. Invite members to share questions or concerns about these issues by writing these comments on paper you will provide. Give 2-3 minutes for them to write out the questions, and then collect them. Begin with this first session training the group members to work together. Explain the four-part approach to sessions: 1. Knowing, 2. Understanding, 3. Experiencing, and 4. Responding. State that each week the group will first review the basic concepts, then resolve questions, share personal application, and finally respond to God in prayer.

4. *Memory Review.* Divide the quads into pairs and have them quote the memory verse and reference until they can do so without prompting. During this time, read over the questions submitted and group together those that are on the same issues.

UNDERSTANDING (20 MIN.)

Start with the questions people seem to have in common and lead a discussion. Point youth to biblical answers by referring to the member book and the Scriptures noted there. Don't feel you need to have all the answers. This first session is a good time for the group to begin looking to you as a partner rather than as the guru—the source of all wisdom—for the group. Don't be afraid to let them see you as a fellow seeker after truth. Don't hesitate to say, "I'm not quite sure about that." You will encourage more group interaction by turning the question back to the group on occasion: "What do you think about that question?" Or, "Let's see if someone can find a Scripture passage that speaks to this."

The purpose here is to clarify biblical truth, not to engage in theological debate, so strictly limit the time. If questions remain, invite the person(s) to speak to you afterward. At that time, if the youth seems to be deeply concerned about the problem, make an appointment to meet together and talk it over. It may be your opportunity to lead him or her toward spiritual growth.

If the group has no pressing questions, this could be an opportunity for you to emphasize an area of truth in unit 1 that means the most to you personally.

BREAK (5 MIN.)

If you are using the two-hour format, take a 5-minute break at this point. Suggest that some may wish to discuss the teachings informally.

EXPERIENCING (20 MIN.)

1. *Reflection.* Ask youth to reflect quietly on the questions on their review sheet and circle the one that was the greatest personal blessing or the most important new insight.

   Now ask members to reflect quietly on the outline and draw a star beside the three greatest personal needs they sense in learning to live more effectively in the power of the Spirit.
2. *Sharing.* In quads, ask volunteers to share their responses to the reflection exercise above. After sufficient time, ask quads to discuss how their understanding of the Spirit and His role in their lives has changed as a result of unit 1.

   Emphasize that sharing should be brief and to the point—not vague generalities like "God blessed me through this study." Rather, "I came to understand why I'm not growing as I should—I've been trying to do it on my own." Or, "My problem is I didn't know such a life existed or how to have it." Make sample responses of your own. Giving a few suggestions on what might be shared will be helpful.
3. *Singing.* Sing together the theme chorus or hymn you have chosen or some other song chosen by the members. If no one in your group seems able to sing (highly unlikely!), do two things. Read the words of the hymn in unison and after the session enlist someone in the group who could learn the hymn before the next session and teach it to the group. Singing is a very important part of experiencing life in the Spirit. You know it's important—we'll be doing it through all eternity!

RESPONDING (20 MIN.)

1. Point out that each week this time will be devoted to our personal commitment to the truths of our study. Ask youth to bow their heads and prayerfully consider making a commitment to pursue life in

the Spirit as a life-long experience. After a couple of minutes, say "Amen" to close the prayer time.

2. In quads, ask each youth to share one way the others can pray for him or her. The request will probably be in line with the testimony given earlier but should not be limited to that. After a youth shares, the other members should pray for that request immediately. Then the next youth can share a request and the others pray. Ask the group to continue praying until everyone has been prayed for. Tell the groups that a person doesn't have to pray aloud unless he or she wants to. As time goes on most members will feel comfortable praying in these groups of three or four people.
3. Suggest that members record in their journals the prayer requests given or other ways you feel you should be praying for fellow members. Remember these requests in your prayer times during the coming week.

Covenant (small group, 10 min.)

Ask youth to turn to page 6 in the member book and read aloud the group covenant. Pray about keeping the covenant. Join hands and pray that God will draw this group into a deeper fellowship with Him and with each other during the coming weeks. Ask each person to pray a one-sentence prayer asking for God's strength and guidance to complete the course and keep this covenant with the other group members. Explain that anyone who doesn't want to pray out loud should feel free to "pass" by simply squeezing the hand of the next person.

Closure (5 min.)

1. Give a brief preview of unit 2. Suggest that members jot down any questions they have at the end of their personal study of the unit and bring them to the small-group session.
2. Offer a closing prayer of praise for the work of the Holy Spirit in our lives, and ask Him to be your Teacher through the coming week.

After the Session

1. Refer to the standard After the Session procedures.
2. If your group had more than 10 members, plan to divide it. Enlist another leader (preferably from those already in the group). If you cannot enlist another leader, consider dividing into 2 groups and meeting at different times during the week.

DESIGNER MODEL

Activity 1: Creating

Session 2 Goals

Youth will:

- describe ways the Holy Spirit created us to be like God
- identify the goal of creation and redemption
- summarize our potential as Christians
- begin to experience daily companionship with God
- commit to pursue life in the Spirit.

Before the Session

- ❑ Refer to standard Before the Session procedures.
- ❑ Gather the following items and include any others you need for activities you may have developed on your own:
  - a copy of Unit 2 Review Quiz (handout 2a) for each member (LG p. 47)
  - prepare the unit review quiz on a transparency, chalkboard, or flipchart.

During the Session

Remember, each time you divide the small group into pairs or quads, give verbal instructions to everyone. If you think they need the help, write the instructions on a chalkboard or newsprint.

Knowing (20 min.)

1. Ask for any written questions.
2. Give each member a copy of Unit 2 Review Quiz (handout 2a) and instruct them to complete the worksheet.
2. *Memory Verse Review.* Divide into pairs for memory work. Remind members that by now they should quote the passage without prompting.

Understanding (40 min.)

1. Regather and ask for answers to the quiz, writing the consensus on the chart you have displayed. Here are my answers:
   1. *experiences life in the Spirit.* "Christlike in behavior" won't do because we should be Christlike in attitudes and thoughts as well as behavior.
   2. *personal; one person of the godhead; uncreated; everywhere present; always present in every believer*
   3. Everything but *body.* Read through the list and get a show of hands on the characteristic members liked best or are most grateful for.
   4. *Loving oneness with God* or something similar. If someone says, "to be like Christ," affirm this; but explain that we must mean by that more than a godly character, we must include being like Christ also in loving oneness with the Father.
   5. All but #2 and #5 because they both anticipate absolute perfection. If there is a difference of opinion on this, explain that there are different views; and we'll study this in more detail later in unit 7. Read through the list, skipping #2 and #5 Ask for a show of hands on the one you most want the Spirit to accomplish in you during this course.
2. Divide into quads and instruct the groups to decide on what issue in the unit was most troublesome and what issue was most encouraging. If groups cannot easily identify the encouraging and troubling issues, invite them to discuss the two questions on page 34 under the heading "The Transformation Connection." Look up Bible passages (from member book or personal knowledge) that provide answers. The recorder in each group should record main points of discussion.
3. Return to full group and ask each group spokesperson (recorder or quad leader or anyone designated by the group) to share their findings. At the conclusion of each presentation, give opportunity for group interaction.
4. If any questions submitted in writing were not covered in previous discussion consider these at this point, beginning with the question most often submitted.

Break (5 min.)

Experiencing (20 min.)

1. Remind youth that at the end of day 5 they were asked to prepare to share from their journals something special the Spirit has taught them or led them to experience. Explain that we need to keep our sharing to no more than two minutes each, so encourage them to speak directly to the point.
2. Sing a theme song or chorus.

Responding (30 min.)

1. Explain that we want to have a time of thanksgiving and praise to the Holy Spirit for who He is and for what He has done in making us God-compatible and for what He is going to do in us. Emphasize that this is a time for thanksgiving and praise, not for petition. To lead a group of people to stick to praise and not slide over into topics of God will be very difficult, but don't give up! Week by week gently lead youth to the place where they will exult in times of sheer praise and thanksgiving. Today will be a good time to start by emphasizing that we want

to concentrate on thanksgiving and praise. Assure them they will have time later to ask the Spirit to do things in their lives. Give 2-4 minutes for reflection on the requests you write on the overhead transparency or chalkboard. Suggest that they refer back to the outline of the unit or the quiz on the unit as a reminder. Write the following topics for your time of thanksgiving and praise:

- *The person of the Holy Spirit* (day 2)
- *Our image* (days 3 and 4)
- *Our capacity/potential as image-bearers of God* (day 5)

2. After reflection ask for volunteers to voice prayers of thanksgiving for each of the three praise items you listed.
3. After the praise time, lead the group in a time of silent prayer, asking the Spirit to do each of the following. After each request pause long enough for them to talk to God about it.
   - make me a truly spiritual person
   - help me understand the Holy Spirit and become an intimate friend of His
   - give me victory over (name of strongest temptation here)
   - help me grow each week into greater likeness to Jesus
   - gain from this course all He has in mind for me
   - bring Him joy today.

Closure (5 min.)

1. Preview unit 3. Remind members to jot down any questions they have at the end of their personal study of the unit and bring them to the small-group session.
2. Close in prayer by expressing your own desire, and then pray for the group as a whole.

After the Session

1. Refer to the standard After the Session procedures.
2. Plan for participant feedback. You will do your group members a service by modeling for them the principle of developing your spiritual gifts by securing evaluation. Use the evaluation form on LG page 40 to request members' evaluation.

THE GREAT UNVEILING

Activity 2: Revelation

Session 3 Goals

Youth will:

- describe what both *inspiration* and *illumination* do and do not mean
- identify the four major ways God reveals His will for us in the Bible
- understand how different approaches affect one's interpretation, especially how "trust and obey" are prerequisites for understanding and applying the Bible
- grow in appreciation for the Spirit's gift of Scripture and His presence to guide us in understanding it.

Before the Session

❑ Refer to the standard Before the Session procedures.

❑ Gather the following items and include any others you need for activities you have developed on your own:

- copies of Unit 3 Review Quiz (handout 3a) and questionnaire (handout 3b) (LG p. 48)
- Unit 3 Review Quiz prepared on a transparency, chalkboard, or flipchart for use in large group time
- a familiar hymn or an appropriate contemporary chorus.

During the Session

Knowing (30 min.)

1. Distribute quiz for the day and collect any written questions members bring.
2. Divide into quads and seek a consensus on the answers to the quiz.
3. *Memory Verse Review.* Divide into pairs and review memory verses.

Understanding (30 min.)

Reconvene the entire group and work through the answers, asking for the consensus of each quad. Here are my answers:

1. False. Many truths are worth knowing that the Bible doesn't deal with; but all the truth we need to know about God, sin, and salvation, for example, are clearly revealed in Scripture.
2. False. A few parts of the Bible are words given directly by God, for example, the Ten Commandments; but most of Scripture is in the language of the human author, reflecting his vocabulary and personality. The Spirit guided the process so that what He wanted communicated was accurate.
3. True. Belief in what we read or hear is based on our believing the author is trustworthy.
4. True.
5. False. Though many treat Scripture as if everyone's interpretation is as good as the next person's, there is only one true interpretation.
6. False. "Illumination" describes the Spirit's work in the reader to help him or her understand the text. "Inspiration" is the term used of the Spirit's work in guiding the biblical author.
7. False. The Bible is supernatural in that it was so inspired by the Holy Spirit that what He wanted to communicate is communicated in straightforward language. His purpose is to reveal truth, not hide it. Though there is picture language in Scripture (figurative language), that too is subject to ordinary rules for understanding language.
8. False. Most of the Bible is clear to those who trust and intend to obey it. Bible believing Christians divide over the interpretation of a small minority of biblical teaching.
9. True.
10. False. We have two things to help us: the Holy Spirit Himself enlightens our minds (illumination) and Spirit-gifted people are given as teachers.
11. True. They might not willingly admit this, but choosing what to believe and what not to believe or obey, is putting personal judgment as the final authority above God's revealed truth.
12. True. Therefore a good degree of modesty about my understanding of difficult or disputed passages is appropriate. Inspiration yields infallibility, illumination does not. Also, I should not be intimidated by those whose interpretation differs from the plain meaning of Scripture, no matter how impressive their credentials.
13. True.
14. False. There may be seven or more ways, depending on how you divide them, but we looked at four important ways to discern God's will in the Bible. Ask members to name them. (Principles, commands, examples of Bible characters—both good and bad, and Jesus' life).
15. True. Therefore, we must be on guard and work hard at finding the intended meaning and not read into the text something from our tradition, culture, or preference. We shall try to do this throughout our study of *Life in the Spirit.*

If any of the questions submitted in advance have not been considered, discuss them now as time permits.

If you're running short of time, invite the person who presented the question(s) to see you after the session.

Break (5 min.)

Suggest they should feel free to continue the discussion during the break.

Experiencing (35 min.)

1. Divide into quads and encourage any member who has struggled with doubts about the trustworthiness of Scripture (or some part of it) or anyone who is now wrestling with the issue to share the story with fellow quad members.
2. While still divided into quads, distribute handout 3b. Instruct members to respond to each item. Then ask them to share what they have written and see if others in the group agree with that analysis.

Responding (15 min.)

1. Remain in quads and pray:
    - for faith to trust and obey the Bible, especially for those still with doubts
    - for Holy Spirit illumination as we study Scripture in this course.
2. Reconvene, distribute the chosen hymn or chorus and sing together in praise of God's wonderful gift of the written revelation of Himself.
3. Spend a few minutes on each of the following topics, suggesting a new topic after several have led in prayer for the last topic presented:
    - Thank the Holy Spirit for revealing all the truth we need to experience God
    - Thank the Holy Spirit for a trustworthy Bible
    - Thank the Holy Spirit that He is our guide in understanding and applying the Bible.

Closure (5 min.)

1. Preview unit 4.
2. In the closing prayer express your own concerns, and then pray for the group.

After the Session

1. Refer to the standard After the Session procedures.
2. If you used student evaluations last week review the responses and see if the changes you made improved this session. Write out any changes that you intend to make next time.

A NEW CREATION

Activity 3: Redeeming

Session 4 Goals

Potential youth members will:

- evaluate whether they have received salvation through Jesus Christ
- describe the activities of the Holy Spirit in the ministry of Jesus
- express the guilt and pain of any unconfessed sin
- describe the wonder of transformation into a new person.

Before the Session

❑ Refer to the standard Before the Session procedures.

❑ Gather the following items:

- a copy of the Unit 4 Review Quiz for each member (handout 4a) (LG p. 49)
- the words to the hymn, "When I Survey The Wondrous Cross."

During the Session

Knowing and Understanding (55 min.)

For today's group session I've combined "Knowing" and "Understanding" because we're dealing with basic truths familiar to most Christians. These truths require special emphasis. The group will explore how the truths relate to the activity of the Holy Spirit.

1. Ask if members have questions they want to have clarified during today's session. Members should have these prepared ahead of time in writing, but if not invite them to jot their questions down now.
2. As members arrive, give them a copy of the Unit 4 Review Quiz (handout 4a). Instruct them to answer only question 1. You will give them instructions as a group for completing questions 2 and 3 of the review.
3. After members have arrived and had a few minutes to complete question 1, lead the group to brainstorm answers to question 1. The group may give all eight activities of the Spirit as covered in the unit, or they may give variations of the described activities. From the list suggested by the members, identify the five core activities related to the ministry of Jesus: empowered Jesus' ministry, accomplished Jesus' death, the conception of Jesus, convicts us of sin, and regeneration. Next give members 5 minutes to complete questions 2 and 3 in the review questions.

   Ask members to discuss their answers to review questions 2 and 3 with their memory work partner.
4. While divided into pairs, quote the memory verse.
5. Return to large group and ask for volunteers to name the activities of the Holy Spirit in order. List them on the chalkboard or transparency. Discuss any questions that remain plus any questions that were submitted to you ahead of class.

My answers to review question 2 are as follows:

1. Jesus' conception by the Spirit comes first because none of the rest could occur without the incarnation.
2. Jesus' ministry (teaching and healing could be divided or combined) and life in the power of the Spirit because without this He could not die as a sinless sacrifice in our place—He would have to die for His own sin.
3. Jesus' death by the Spirit to provide for our salvation, without which the conviction of sin would be meaningless torment and regeneration impossible.
4. Conviction of sin by the Spirit which precedes repentance and faith, both of which are required for regeneration.
5. Regeneration, the Holy Spirit's "recreation" of the believing sinner who cries out for salvation.

Break (5 min.)

Experiencing (30 min.)

1. Read each verse of the hymn, "When I Survey the Wondrous Cross" in unison and pause briefly for reflection between each verse.
2. *Testimony time.*
   a. Ask for volunteers to share briefly their conversion experience (a few sentences, not the whole history).
   b. Ask for volunteers to share specific ways in which they found themselves transformed into what they weren't before—and couldn't have been!
   c. Ask for volunteers to share an experience of conviction of sin and repentance. Also, some might have had an experience of a sense of guilt when not actually guilty. If someone shares such an experience, ask for the way he came to understand he was not guilty.
3. Sing together the hymn "When I Survey the Wondrous Cross."

Responding (25 min.)

1. Lead the group in a time of silent prayer. Guide members to pray for the following:

a. Think of some sin the Holy Spirit has been convicting you of lately, even now. Confess it and ask forgiveness. Thank Him for Jesus' blood that atoned for that very sin. Tell Him how sorry you are for causing Him pain. Allow at least 2 minutes for silent prayer.

b. Think of several changes you couldn't have made on your own. Thank Him for transforming you into a different kind of person. Allow time for reflection and prayer.

c. Ask, **Have you ever repented and trusted God to forgive you on the merits of Christ and make you His child? If you've never done that or you aren't sure that you have, do it now as we silently pray together. You might pray something like this: "Father, I've sinned against You and don't deserve to be Your child. Please forgive me and make me Your child. Thank You. I now give my whole life over to You and ask You to take charge and remake me into Your own image. I trust You to keep Your word and save me for all eternity."**

2. Close the prayer with a time of thanksgiving; seek to voice the sentiments your group expressed as they prayed silently. After praying, ask the group if any prayed to receive Christ. Say, **If you've prayed such a prayer, Jesus said the angels in heaven are throwing a great celebration *(Luke 15:10)*. We want to rejoice with you, too.** Invite any members who prayed to receive Christ to share their decision with the group. Allow time for members to respond. If one or more share, ask for volunteers to pray for the those who have made or confirmed their decision.

Closure (5 min.)

1. Preview unit 5. Suggest that members jot down any questions they have at the end of their personal study of the unit and bring them to the next small-group session.
2. Offer a closing prayer of praise for the work of the Holy Spirit in our lives, and ask Him to be our teacher through the coming week.

After the Session

Refer to the standard After the Session procedures.

CLOSE CONNECTION

Session 5 Goals

Youth will:
- describe the hurt God feels when we refuse to trust Him
- identify what unbelief does to the Christian
- commit to experience obedience as an aspect of faith
- understand the place of law in the life of a believer
- express gratitude for God's law.

Before the Session

❑ Refer to standard Before the Session procedures.
❑ Gather four large sheets of paper with the headings found in handout 5a (LG p. 50).

During the Session

Arrival Activity (10 min.)

1. Collect any written questions youth may have.
2. As members arrive ask them to complete each sentence in handout 5a.
3. *Memory Verse Review.* Instruct members to complete memory work as their partners arrive.

Knowing (20 min.)

1. Ask each of the following questions of the group. List answers on a transparency or chalkboard as they voice them; then discuss and/or vote on an answer before moving to the next question.
   a. As a believer, who lives inside you?
   b. What am I saying about God when I don't trust Him?
   c. What is the relationship between "trust" and "obedience"?
   d. What's so bad about disobedience? What does it do to me? What does it do to God?
   e. How does the purpose of law in the life of a non-believer differ from the purpose of law for a believer?

   In the discussion, try to lead the members to recall the following teachings from this unit:
   a. All three members of the Trinity live in me.
   b. When I don't trust God I call into question His character, especially His wisdom, power, or love.
   c. Trust and obedience are two aspects of saving and sanctifying faith. To be saved a person needs to repent and believe; to grow, a Christian must yield and trust. Some believe that repentance (in the unbeliever) and yielding (in the believer) are not part of faith but the necessary evidence of true faith. Either way, to be connected with God in a close relationship we need both.
   d. Disobedience disconnects. Disobedience does not disconnect us from God's saving grace, but it always puts distance between us and God—"breaking fellowship." No possibility of a close connection exists for the disobedient child of God. (Some might indicate how disobedience affects God, which is OK even if we covered that in 2d).
   e. For the non-believer the law condemns—it's God's method of leading persons to see their need of salvation. For the believer, however, *"There is now no condemnation for those who are in Christ Jesus," (Rom. 8:1);* but we still need the law. It's God's will for us, describing the goal—to be like Him. In that sense the law is a light on our spiral up, showing us the right way and the wrong way. You might say the law is a light over the mirror to show us how sinful we are when out of Christ. It becomes a headlight for those in Christ to see the way to go.

Understanding (35 min.)

1. Divide into quads and have each group seek a consensus on each pair of questions they answered on arrival.
2. Regather and have each group report their choices for interaction by the whole group. Be sure the following emphases come through clearly and that any questions submitted on arrival are covered. Whenever a written question isn't addressed in class be sure to contact the youth later and try to meet his or her concern.
   a. "For Christ to be in me means ..." In some mysterious way Christ is present in my body, but our emphasis in this unit is that His indwelling means the relationship has the potential of being very close.
   b. "For me to be in Christ means ..." To be in Christ has a judicial aspect in that He is the substitute for me, taking the judgment due me; but, like Christ being in me, my being in Him also emphasizes the intimate relationship I now have. Both "in's" are the in's of fellowship.
   c. "What I like about the law is ..." Law is necessary to show us what we'll be like when we're like Jesus, so it's as welcome as a flashlight on a dark path. If I don't love it, I must have trouble with obedience. Or I could be misusing it—allowing it to stand in condemnation of me like an unbeliever, or trying to obey it to become acceptable to God. We are acceptable to God

on the merits of Christ alone. But the law now serves as a guide for Christian living, giving us concrete instruction on how our love for God and others will prompt us to think and behave.

d. We can know clearly whether we're connected with God by our obedience. But a close connection, intimate companionship and a sense of oneness with Him depend on our trust in Him. The obedience we can choose or refuse and in that sense we're either "connected" or not. Obedience is the evidence of genuine faith. But in trust we grow through companioning with God, "keeping step with the Spirit" as we experience His work in our lives.

3. Now is the time to review the first five units to be sure youth see the connections among them, the development of our theme of *Life in the Spirit*. To prepare for this exercise, a quick review can be found in unit 1. Point to the unit titles on your course outline and ask how each prepares for or relates to the next. One way to do this would be to review the activities of the Holy Spirit. Point out on the course map the place of each activity.

a. The Spirit created us in God's image (unit 2) so we can love and be loved by Him, but we broke that bond of love by choosing our own way. In this we lost our way and stumbled downward toward even greater destruction, but...

b. God revealed a way back by showing us what He is like and how we can return (unit 3). The Spirit did this through prophets and apostles in the Bible. But He did more than that.

c. The Spirit was instrumental in each step of Jesus' incarnation, providing for our salvation; and it is He who convicts us of our need of a Savior, of our need to make the big turn-around and trust Him. Whether faith comes first or regeneration, the Holy Spirit is the one who makes us into altogether new people—once again God-compatible. Even more, He comes to live with us in person (unit 4). Problem is, we may not stay in a close relationship with Him, so we need...

d. To yield again to His absolute rule. We must trust Him (unit 5) to begin again the transforming work, spiraling us up toward greater likeness to Jesus and closer companionship with Him. We'll look more closely at that activity of the Spirit in unit 6.

Break (5 min.)

Experiencing (25 min.)

1. Sing a familiar hymn such as "Trust and Obey."
2. Ask for a show of hands on who has had an experience of "re-connecting," coming back into a close relationship with God after drifting or rebellion.
3. Ask for any who would share briefly that experience. Don't let the time get away from you here! If your group is quite vocal (some members are) you might suggest they give a summary of their experience in a few sentences.
4. Sing a praise hymn like "Abide with Me," or a chorus like "Sweet, Sweet, Spirit."

Responding (20 min.)

1. Guided private prayer.

a. Ask members to meet with God in making a commitment or reaffirming a commitment to yield unconditionally to His will. Suggest that if they have had some barrier to fellowship with God they be specific in telling God exactly what it is.

b. Ask members to reflect on how they felt when someone they loved didn't trust them. Pause for a few moments, then suggest they tell the Lord how sorry they are for hurting Him by doubting His wisdom, power, or love. Suggest that they name the specific matter in which they struggled with doubt and the specific characteristic of God they questioned.

c. Now lead them to thank God for His wisdom, power, and love and ask for daily growth in trusting.

d. Now ask members to express aloud prayers of gratitude for God's presence within, for who He is. Suggest that they mention specific things about God for which they are grateful. One way to do this would be to suggest that they pray a single sentence or even just a single word of praise, feeling free to pray again and again as the Spirit lifts their spirits in exalting God.

Closure (5 min.)

1. Preview unit 6.
2. Offer a closing prayer of thanksgiving for the glorious life of intimate companionship with Him that the Spirit promises.

After the Session

Refer to the standard After the Session procedures.

SPIRALING UP

Activity 5: Transforming

SESSION 6 GOALS

Youth will:

- affirm that they have made the "turn around"
- express their commitment to the devotional life by planning for improving their time spent with God
- reevaluate the role of the church in their personal growth
- identify the two most basic reasons for personal pain: God's glory and my growth.

BEFORE THE SESSION

❑ Refer to standard Before the Session procedures.

❑ Gather the following items and include any others you need for activities you may have developed on your own:

- copies of Unit 6 Review Quiz (handout 6a) and Concept Checkup (handout 6b) (LG p. 50-51) for each member.

DURING THE SESSION

KNOWING (25 MIN.)

1. Collect any written questions youth brought with them.
2. Give each youth a copy of Unit 6 Review Quiz (handout 6a) and ask them to answer these while others are arriving.
3. Allow about 10 minutes for completing the review and then go over the answers to 1-3, putting them on the overhead or chalkboard as the group responds.
   1. Any word that means a turning will do, words like *repentance, reconsecration, yielding to God.* Be sure they understand that this is true of anyone, believer or unbeliever, who would follow Jesus. Without that unconditional yes of the heart, there can be no genuine spiritual growth.
   2. We discussed the Bible, prayer, church, and suffering as means of grace. If any youth leave off *suffering* or *adversity* as a means of growth, now would be a great opportunity to point out that hardship can actually provide the fast track for growth.
   3. Ignorance, unyieldedness (through either drift or rebellion), and unbelief (lack of trust). Synonyms will do, of course.
   4. *Memory Verse Review.* Divide into pairs for memory passage review.

Understanding (30 min.)

1. Distribute the Concept Checkup exercise (handout 6b) and allow members 7 minutes to answer. Allow at least 10-15 minutes to interact on these questions designed to help members understand the implications of what we've been thinking about. Here are my answers:
   1. I marked all of them false. Either true or false is OK for item *c,* but we want to emphasize that surrender is a decision. On item *d* remind them of the memory verse, "make every effort to add to your faith ...." Faith, though some must be present, is something we must grow all our lives. Also, on the surrender side, you could say we grow in understanding new areas to surrender and in strength to overcome. But we need to emphasize the basic orientation that it's either yes to God or no when it comes to yielding to His will. It will be helpful if members focus on a decision for surrender and growth in faith or trust. The key word in item e is behavior. We must grow in Christlike attitudes as well as in Christlike behavior. But even more important we must remind our youth that the ultimate goal is loving oneness with God, not merely good conduct. Good behavior is not the final goal.
   2. Faith.
   3. I didn't strike out any—trouble can come from any of those sources.
   4. Though any of those in the list may sometimes be in God's purpose, those always present are the glory of God and my growth toward Christlikeness.

BREAK (5 MIN.)

EXPERIENCING (30 MIN.)

1. Divide into quads and ask members (those who wish to) to read their answer to #4 of review quiz—their own story of spiraling up.
2. Return to full group and invite those who will to share one or two experiences from their lives—
   - a "turnaround" experience or
   - a "blessed adversity" experience—some heartache or pain that God turned into an opportunity to display His power in delivering or in giving strength to endure. Or how some suffering brought about spiritual growth.
3. Sing a familiar hymn like "I Surrender All," "Have Thine Own Way, Lord," or a chorus like "He Is Lord."

Responding (20 min.)

1. Private prayer. This time of prayer should be guided by the leader. Following each suggestion, give members time to pray concerning that issue. Lead the group to pray about—
   - Surrender—Make sure you have chosen to turn your life over to God or reaffirm that commitment.
   - Commitment to faithful devotional time each day. Ask forgiveness for failure if needed.
   - Gratitude for the church and renewal of the vows you made at baptism. Commitment to being accountable, perhaps beginning an accountability partner relationship.
   - Acceptance of any present pain or hard times in faith that God is in it. Give thanks for the outcome He promises, if not for the sorrow itself.
2. Divide into quads and suggest each one share in turn any concern coming from this unit's activities—strength needed to change, gratitude for specific new light, hope for accelerated growth pattern. After each one shares, the person to his or her left (or right) should pray briefly for that request.

Closure (10 min.)

1. Read in unison the original covenant signed in the first session.
2. Preview unit 7.
3. Offer a closing prayer of thanksgiving for the glorious life the Spirit provides.

After the Session

Refer to the standard After the Session procedures.

EXPECTATIONS

Session 7 Goals

Unlike previous sessions, the goal of this session is primarily understanding.

Youth will:

- describe what they can expect from living life in the Spirit
- determine biblical definitions of sin, perfection, victory, and faith.

Before the Session

❑ Refer to the standard Before the Session procedures.

❑ Gather the following items and include any others you need for activities you have developed on your own:

- a copy of the Unit 7 Review Quiz (handout 7a) for each member (LG p. 52)
- a copy of the Biblical Balance Chart (handout 7b) for each member (LG p. 53)
- a flipchart, chalkboard, or markerboard with *Varieties of Sin* written at the top and three columns with the headings:
  1. *deliberate or willful;*
  2. *unintentional;*
  3. *resulting from slavery.*
- a flipchart, chalkboard, or poster displaying the outline for victorious Christian living: *God's Standard, God's Provision,* and *My Responsibility.*

During the Session

Knowing (25 min.)

1. Collect any questions members have written out and brought with them. Give each person a copy of the unit 7 review questions (handout 7a).
2. Memory Verse Review. Instruct members to pair off when they have completed the review questions and review all the memory work from units 1-7.

Understanding (60 min.)

1. Reconvene the group and note the answers to the review on the chalkboard or transparency, referring back to days 5, 3, or 4 if necessary. For activities of the Spirit, point out how each fits in the course outline.
2. Point to the short summary course outline on a transparency or chalkboard. Say, **You will remember we began in unit 1 with this outline for the victorious Christian life:**
   - **God's Standard (for Christian Living),**
   - **God's Provision (for Christian Living),**
   - **My Responsibility (to use that provision).**

   Ask the youth for one-word definitions of each and write the answers beside the statements. (Our standard is either God or Jesus; Our provision is the (Holy) Spirit; My responsibility is faith.)
3. State: **Successful Christian living must involve a balanced view of these resources. To describe God's standard, God's provision, and my responsibility in a balanced way is difficult. Here is an exercise that asks you to identify some examples of imbalanced thinking and then to write a statement of balance. Please take 5-10 minutes to complete the exercise.** Distribute handout 7b and point out how each expectancy relates to the course summary outline you've just noted.

Break (5 min.)

Continuing "Understanding"

4. Reconvene and ask what quads concluded regarding biblical balance in expectations. Lead members to share their statements. If possible write a consensus statement of expectation under each category before reading my statement.

   1. My responses for #1 were: a, H; b, L; c, L; d, H. For my statement, I wrote: "God's plan is for me to spiral up into greater likeness to Jesus in my attitudes and actions. In the conscious choices, the new me with the indwelling Spirit's power can consistently choose right."
   2. My responses for #2 were: a, SE; b, NE; c, NE; d, SE. For my statement I wrote: "I don't have what it takes to live successfully, so the Holy Spirit provides all the resources for this victory and growth. But He expects me to work with Him in faithfully using the means of grace.
   3. My responses for #3 were: a, P; b, F; c, P; d, F. For my statement I wrote: "Sanctifying faith is trusting God to do what He has promised, not what He hasn't promised; and then acting on that in obedience, not simply resigning myself to my fate."
5. Lead the group in completing the following exercise designed to help distinguish the three varieties of sin for which we have different expectancies: (a) deliberate or willful, (b) unintentional, (c) resulting from slavery.

   On a flipchart, chalkboard, or markerboard write *Varieties of Sin* at the top and make three columns with these headings:

1. deliberate or willful;
2. unintentional;
3. resulting from slavery

Call out each of the following words and list each under one of the three columns as participants give answers (I have included my answers in parentheses):

willful (1)	inadvertent (2)
premeditated (1)	planned (1)
involuntary (3)	unwitting (2)
unknown (2)	impulse (3)
choice (1)	sins of disposition (2 or 3)

6. If any of the questions or problems members submitted on arrival at the session have not been covered in the discussions thus far, consider them now before going on.

EXPERIENCING (5 MIN.)

Sing a familiar hymn on victory.

RESPONDING (20 MIN.)

1. Divide into quads. Invite members to share whether they asked someone the question, "If you could change one thing about me, what would it be?" If the quads have bonded sufficiently by now, perhaps those who didn't ask anyone that question would like to reflect on why they didn't and share that reason with the others.
2. The time of prayer should be thanksgiving for the expectations God has given us and intercession for God to give the victory. If the small group has bonded well, they could pray specifically about what they're trusting God to give victory in.

CLOSURE (5 MIN.)

1. Preview unit 8.
2. Close with a prayer of thanksgiving for the glorious life the Spirit provides.

AFTER THE SESSION

Refer to the standard After the Session procedures.

FILLED FULL

Activity 6: Filling

Session 8 Goals

Youth will:
- describe the three meanings of full
- evaluate their fullness in the first meaning of the term (unconditional lordship)
- express their desire and hope for being filled in the second meaning of the term (abundant crop of fruit and power in ministry)
- build an awareness of fullness in the third meaning of the term (a strong subjective sense of His presence)
- commit to pray for revival.

Before the Session

❑ Refer to standard Before the Session procedures.

❑ Gather the following items and include any others you need for activities you may have developed on your own:
- copies of Unit 8 Review Quiz (handout 8a), True or False Quiz (handout 8b), and Prayer Guide (handout 8c) for each member (LG p. 54-55).

During the Session

Knowing (20 min.)

1. Collect any written questions youth brought with them.
2. Give youth a copy of Unit 8 Review Quiz (handout 8a) and ask them to answer these while others are arriving.
3. *Memory Verse Review.* When they have completed the review, instruct them to pair off and review the memory verses for unit 8.

Be sure all members can recall the three meanings before moving on to Understanding.

Understanding (20 min.)

1. Distribute the Unit 8 True or False Quiz (handout 8b). Allow 3-4 minutes to write answers, and then ask members to divide into pairs and discuss their answers. Then regroup and ask for answers from the group. Interact on each answer and consider any questions that haven't been dealt with. My answers would be:
   1. False. Others best judge whether my life reflects Christlike characteristics. Though I should regularly evaluate my own growth and try to be honest about it, I may be the poorest judge. In fact, if I feel I'm full of fruit it could be evidence of the opposite—pride!
   2. True. Revival means to have life again, it refers first of all to those who have life and in whom the fire may have died down—Christians. We usually use the term to refer to what happens to a group of believers, though the same could be said of an individual.
   3. True. Give a word of encouragement to have this hope for themselves personally.
   4. True. This experience happened often to the early disciples—these Spirit-filled people were said to be "filled." A mystery remains in the term *filled*, after all our study and analysis.
   5. False. The first and last meanings—unconditional yieldedness and inner feelings—are the only two the person can know for sure. Others, however, are the best judge of whether a person is full of fruit or gifts, the second meaning of the term.
   6. True. Not only true, but the only place fullness can begin. Yielding starts the flow of the Spirit's full power.
   7. False. Point out on the course outline how most of the course thus far has been about our growth in greater likeness to Christ in the way we think and behave. Instead of your giving the answers, you might ask youth to describe how each unit you point to is related to fruit.

Experiencing (40 min.)

1. Invite youth to tell something supernatural they have observed in the life or ministry of someone else in the group. If that moves slowly, broaden the invitation to include anyone in their church they have observed.
2. Ask youth to tell briefly some experience they have had of fullness in any of the three senses of full: (1) turning life over to God unconditionally, (2) special victory over temptation or surge of power in ministry, and (3) inner sense of God's presence so strong the joy or some other emotion can't be described. You were so full you felt you'd overflow—and maybe you did with tears, song, or words of praise.
3. Sing a familiar hymn like "Revive Us Again," or a chorus like "Search Me, O God."

Break (5 min.)

Responding (30 min.)

1. Distribute the Prayer Guide for the prayer time and instruct the leader of each quad to move to the next suggested item for prayer when it seems

appropriate. Divide into quads for prayer after you lead them in #1.

CLOSURE (5 MIN.)

1. Preview unit 9.
2. Close with prayer of thanksgiving for the glorious hope of being constantly filled with the Spirit.

AFTER THE SESSION

Refer to the standard After the Session activities.

BATTLE PLAN

Activity 7: Overcoming

Session 9 Goals

Youth will:
- recall causes of temptation and root sins
- describe defensive and offensive use of the Bible, prayer, and the church
- express growing hope that they can overcome temptation.

Before the Session

❑ Refer to standard Before the Session procedures.
❑ Gather the following items and include any others you need for activities you may have developed on your own:
- one slip of paper with each of the following words or phrases: Inner desires, impulses, lust, God, Satan, covetousness, desire to enjoy, circumstances, pride, desire to have, other people, unbelief, desire to be significant, self love
- 3 columns on the chalkboard, poster, or a transparency with the following headings: 1. Sources of Temptation, 2. Root Sins, 3. Neither Source nor Root
- on a chalkboard, poster, or transparency write the following chart on battle strategy:
  1. Desire to do God's will and surrender to His leadership
  2. Identify the source of temptation
  3. Recognize the root sin
  4. Make your choice

During the Session

Knowing (20 min.)

1. Collect any written questions youth brought with them.
2. Give each member one or two of the slips of paper you prepared. Ask them to place each slip under one of the three columns: 1. Sources of Temptation, 2. Root Sins, 3. Neither Source nor Root.
3. Memory Work Review. When they have placed their word or words under one of the columns, instruct them to pair off and review the memory verses for unit 9.
4. Ask if youth agree on what has been put under each of the three columns. Discuss any differences of opinion to be sure all youth know the possibilities. Here are my answers:

Sources of Temptation	*Root Sins*	*Neither Source or Root Sins*
inner desires, impulses	lust	God
Satan	covetousness	desire to enjoy
circumstances	pride	desire to have
other people	unbelief	desire to be significant
	self-love	self-love

Note that self-love could be under Root Sins or Neither, depending on other factors. Loving oneself is no sin; but when love for self overrides love for God or others, it becomes a root sin, perhaps the basic sin from which all others grow.

Understanding (45 min.)

To help understand the battle strategy, work through a case study. First tell this story: Mary's dad didn't pick her up from school on time, and Mary blew up again. Mary has a habit of losing her temper when things don't go her way. Without checking to see why her dad was running late, she assumed he was at fault. She wants to stop this kind of reaction to her dad. Use the battle strategy chart you prepared earlier to illustrate the strategy.

1. What good start has Mary already made? (She really wants God's will, knows she is sinning and admits it, at least to herself.)
2. Mary needs to identify the source of her temptation. From where is it coming? Let group give answers and write them on chalkboard or transparency.
   - Mary's Dad. (Doesn't help much in solving the problem. If Mary concentrates her anger on her dad by blaming or faulting him, she will excuse or rationalize her behavior and fail to grow!)
   - Circumstances. (Obviously so, especially if she had a hard day at school or if she had a friend riding home with her. Still, that doesn't do much to solve her temper problem since there will always be aggravating circumstances.)
   - Satan. (Maybe so, particularly if the enemy has an interest in destroying that relationship or in exploiting Mary's weak spot to bring her down spiritually.)
   - God. (She may be tempted to blame God for giving her this dad. God isn't the source of temptation. He has permitted it, for at least two reasons: His glory and Mary's growth.)
   - Herself. (This is the bottom line. If Mary didn't respond out of what's on the inside, none of the other sources could have tempted her successfully. Point out that blame-laying and finger-pointing—finding the source outside herself—may not help much. So move on to the next source—what is the root sin that lies behind Mary losing her

temper?)

3. What possible reasons or root sins cause Mary to blow up? Ask youth for answers, writing them down. It would help for them to explain their answers.
   - Lust. (Perhaps Mary is involved with a young man her dad wouldn't approve. The closer she gets to him, the more irritated she is with her dad.)
   - Covetousness. (She just started hanging out with this new friend and was hoping her dad's new car would impress her.)
   - Pride. (It hurts to admit her problem with temper and self-centeredness.)
   - Unbelief. (Certainly a factor—she's not trusting God to help her love her dad, and she's not trusting the Spirit to direct her dad.)
   - Self-love. (Mary just plain loves herself more than she loves her dad, doesn't want to be inconvenienced, doesn't care about his feelings.)

   Point out that if Mary is to wage war on her temper, she needs to identify one or more root causes and attack those–not just the nasty temper. Maybe she isn't altogether sure about the source or the root of her temptation, however. Can she still win out? How?
4. What should she do? On a markerboard or tearsheet write the two headings: offensive strategies and defensive strategies. Ask members to brainstorm possible actions Mary can take to deal with her temper. (See pp. 116-122).

BREAK (5 MIN.)

EXPERIENCING (30 MIN.)

Divide into quads and invite members to share the personal strategy they developed in day 5. When the groups seem to be winding down or when the time is up, bring them together and encourage them to follow through on their beginning and develop a full-blown strategy. Have them set a specific time to work on their plan.

RESPONDING (15 MIN.)

1. Sing a hymn like, "Victory In Jesus" or "I Surrender All."
2. Ask youth to pray aloud for themselves and for one another, asking for victory in the battle against temptation, especially those temptations which have been winning out. Claim the victory in prayer!

CLOSURE (5 MIN.)

1. Preview unit 10.
2. Offer a closing prayer of thanksgiving for the victory we can have in the battle.

AFTER THE SESSION

Refer to the standard After the Session procedures.

THE SPIRIT'S GIFTS

Activity 8: Gifting

SESSION 10 GOALS

Youth will:

- describe the relationship between the gifts of the Spirit, the fruit of the Spirit, the tasks in the church, the offices in the church, and natural talents
- identify gift needs in their church(es)
- develop or increase their desire for a greater ministry or greater ministry effectiveness
- begin or continue the process of developing their Spirit-given abilities.

BEFORE THE SESSION

❑ Refer to the standard Before the Session procedures.

❑ Gather the following items and include any others you need for activities you have developed.

- For the following activity, I have assembled a representative list of seven spiritual gifts. Prepare slips of paper, each with one of the seven gifts. The ability to—

1. teach the Bible
2. win people to Christ
3. meet human needs
4. counsel
5. preach with authority
6. lead effectively
7. administrate

- Write on a tearsheet, or marker board as follows:

Strongly expressed in my church		*Weakly expressed in my church*
	worship	
	fellowship	
	discipleship	
	ministry	
	evangelism	
	all the purposes	

- Supply pins, tape, chalk, or markers to write or attach the slips to the chart
- Make copies of handouts 10a and 10b (LG p. 56)
- Secure a copy of *Experiencing God, Youth Edition* workbook.

DURING THE SESSION

KNOWING (25 MIN.)

1. Collect any written questions youth brought.
2. Give each member a gift name. If you have more than seven members, you'll need to make duplicates of some gift or gifts. Depending on the medium you use, provide pins, tape, chalk, or markers. Instruct members to place or write the gift names on the list of purposes of the church where they are needed to accomplish that purpose. Instruct them to place the gift to the side of the chart that indicates the gift is either strongly or weakly expressed in their church.
3. Memory Verse Review. When members have attached their gifts, instruct them to pair off and review the memory verses for unit 10 and the previous memory verses.
4. Seek a group consensus on the following questions. Tell them it's an "open book" quiz—they can check their workbook for answers.

1. Are all gifts of equal importance? What is your reason for that answer?

Possible answers include:

a. In *1 Corinthians 12* and *14* the Bible teaches the gifts are of very different importance. Some are more valuable than others to God in fulfilling His purposes in the church and in the world.

b. The most important gift for me is the one God has given me or would give me.

c. The most important thing for the church is for all members to fulfill the function God designed for them.

2. What is more important than any gift? (1 Cor. 12:31–13:3)

3. Does a great gift mean great spirituality? (Probe this one—the relationship between "fruit" and "gift" and the fact that "spirituality" refers to fruit. Point out on the course outline how the subjects have been about personal growth toward greater likeness to Jesus.)

4. Does a great gift mean great reward? (Reward is based on faithfulness, including faithfulness with one's gift. Faithfulness is a "fruit.")

5. How do we know what gifts are available?

a. The Bible lists gifts and examples (you may want to point out four gift lists in the New Testament listed on page 129. However, not many are defined in Scripture.)

b. Needs the church has to fulfill its purposes. (If we seek the Spirit-given ability to meet the need and fulfill the purpose, we may find the giftedness God supplies includes natural talent, experience, and learning, as well as identifiable spiritual gifts. All abilities are, in the final analysis, gifts the Spirit supplies.)

6. What are some ways I can develop my gift? In each

of the following, ask for any available examples members might be acquainted with:

a. involvement—try it out
b. apprentice/mentor
c. literature/media
d. special training
e. interchurch seminars
f. formal training

Understanding (20 min.)

1. Distribute copies of handout 10a, the purposes of the church and gifts that contribute to those purposes. Seek a consensus on which gifts go with which purpose, helping members understand the relationship between gift and purpose.
2. Explain that for purpose of discussion we have used the seven examples I supplied. Now broaden the discussion to include all the gifts included in the New Testament gift lists. Refer to page 129 as necessary. Seek to lead the group to identify the ministry purpose of the gifts and relate the gifts to the ministry of the church.

Break (5 min.)

Experiencing (40 min.)

1. Refer back to the original responses members gave on the purposes-of-the-church chart. Seek a consensus among members as to which purposes are being achieved in their church and which need the strength of additional gifts to achieve them. If your group is from different churches, divide into same-church groups for this exercise. Otherwise, do it all together.

   If the group reaches agreement on certain needs, ask for suggestions on what to do about it. Possible answers include:
   - We need to seek out people who might fill the gaps or who might develop the necessary gifts.
   - We need to pray more diligently for God to supply the gifts.
   - We need to more actively mentor people to help them discover their gifts.
2. Ask for testimonials of those who have had or have been a mentor in developing abilities. To prompt response, refer to the challenge in day 4, page 133 about seeking a mentor or reaching out to be a mentor. You might ask for a show of hands as to who followed through on that suggestion or who intends to.
3. Explain that the course, *Experiencing God, Youth Edition,* is a wonderful resource for putting this unit into practice. If youth have taken that course, ask for specific correlation between the principles of this unit on gifts and discovering what God is doing and joining Him in that. If they haven't done that course, recommend that they do so at the earliest opportunity.

Responding (25 min.)

1. Read the words of Frances Ridley Havergal's magnificent hymn, "Lord, Speak to Me, That I May Speak" (handout 10b). Then sing it as a prayer.
2. Divide into quads if all are from the same church or by church group and pray for those areas of needed gifts in the church.
3. Divide into pairs and ask each to share what gift(s) they truly desire for God's glory in the church and then pray for each other.
4. Ask each person to check day 4, page 134 (the personal plan to seek and/or develop some gift he desires, or a gift needed in his church), and update it in the light of this group session activity.

Closure (5 min.)

1. Preview unit 11.
2. Offer a closing prayer of thanksgiving for the wonderful gifts the Spirit gives His church.

After the Session

1. If all of your group is from your own church, do you have any results from today's activities that should be called to the attention of the church leadership? Is there any other action you might take to help your church maximize the potential in your people for greater participation in accomplishing the purposes of the church? Any people you need to recruit for specific tasks? Someone who needs mentoring that you might provide?

   ____

   ____

   ____

   ____
2. Refer to the standard After the Session procedures.

POWER TO CHANGE THE WORLD

Activity 9: Sending

Session 11 Goals

Youth will:

- describe the biblical basis of missions
- distinguish between the responsibility to witness and the gift of evangelism
- identify the characteristics of a truly "Great Commission" church
- evaluate the current state of the world from God's viewpoint
- commit to an additional growth step in witnessing, praying, and giving.

Before the Session

❑ Refer to standard Before the Session procedures.

❑ This session involves more handouts and charts than usual. Prepare the following items:

- a simple diagram on newsprint, chalkboard, or transparency to represent the following:

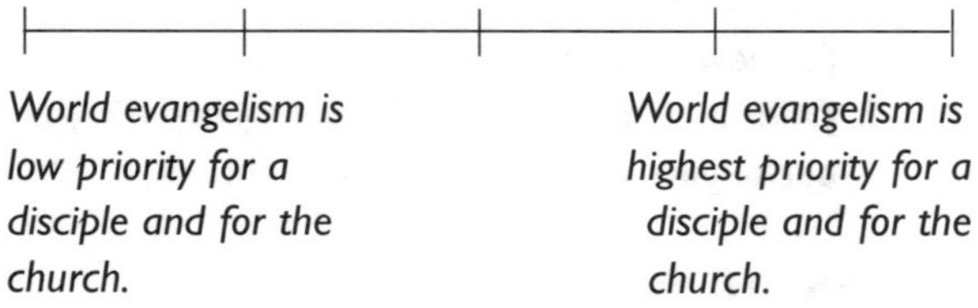

- a copy of each of the following for each member:

The Progress of World Evangelism (handout 11a) (LG p. 57)

"10/40 Window" map (handout 11b) (LG p. 58)

"Great Commission Church Profile" (handout 11c) (LG p. 59). Note that you may need to find answers to this exercise ahead of time—from the church office or pastor.

"My Great Commission Investment" (handout 11d) (LG p. 60).

During the Session

Knowing (20 min.)

1. Collect any written questions youth brought.
2. As youth arrive give the following instructions for the world-evangelism chart above: On the diagram displayed put a star (*) on the place you feel God would have voted in the debate between the theologian and the missions leader (see unit 11 introduction), then initial the place you believe you are yourself as demonstrated by your attitudes and actions. Put an *X* at the place you think your church might be. Then write on the chart your reasons to believe God's attitude toward world evangelism is what you chose.
3. Divide into twos and review the memory verse.
4. Display the scale you prepared before class on the importance of world evangelism. Ask members to come to a group consensus about where God would vote in the debate between the theologian and the missions leader and place a *G* on the scale. Then say to the group, Initial the place you believe you are as demonstrated by your attitudes and actions. Put an *X* on the place where you think your church might be.
5. Divide into quads. Instruct each group of four to combine their reasons why God places a high priority on world evangelism. Each group is to come up with a summary statement of those reasons (see day 1: God's Character, God's Activity, God's Promises, Christ's Command). After about 10 minutes ask each group to vote on whether those reasons are sufficient to warrant our devoting a whole unit of study to the single gift of evangelism.
6. Reconvene and get a report from each group, both on their list of reasons and their vote. Write reasons on transparency, chalkboard, or poster as they are given. Guide a brief discussion of their answers.

Understanding (35 min.)

1. Devote no more than 20 minutes to discussing the following three questions. The discussion could go on forever, but limit the time devoted to this exercise.

   a. *Is the distinction the author made between witness and an evangelistic gift biblically valid?*

   b. *What personal changes would you make if you believed you were sinning if you did not win many people to faith?*
   (Possible answers include: guilt; discouragement; witness less; I should feel guilty because everyone should win people to Christ; I should feel guilty because I do have the gift of evangelism but am not using it well. You'll notice that I think all those possible answers are valid except "guilt because everyone should win people to Christ.")

   c. *How would church prayer times, training programs, and expectations be different if all church leaders believed that every member is called to be a faithful witness, but not all are given the gift of evangelism?*
   (Possible answers: sermons leave people feeling guilty only if they don't witness, not if they are unsuccessful in praying with many people to

receive Christ; training would be for everyone in being more effective witnesses, only some for more effective evangelism; emphasis would be on "body life evangelism"—many members participating in various ways in winning a person to faith.)

2. Distribute copies of the "The Progress of World Evangelism" chart (handout 11a). Divide into quads. Ask members to decide on where the church as a whole should put its greatest emphasis on evangelism—world A, B, C, or D. After 5 minutes distribute "10/40 Window" chart (handout 11b) and point out where we are actually investing our resources.

Break (5 min.)

Experiencing (25 min.)

1. Divide into quads and spend 10 minutes in prayer for the missionaries known to members and for the unreached peoples of the world. Depending on how knowledgeable members are, you may need to introduce some missionaries and their ministry. If they don't know any missionaries sufficiently to pray for them, you might ask who followed through on the suggestion on page 145 to find and "adopt" at least one missionary.
2. Regather and sing several missionary hymns or choruses such as "Rescue the Perishing" or "People Need the Lord."
3. Distribute the chart on a "Great Commission Church" (handout 11c) and ask them to put a check to mark the ideal biblical church and an *X* by where their own church is. Also, display the chart so you can mark on it the consensus reached following discussion.

   The Bible reveals no official "right" answers, but in the light of God's revealed heart and purpose for this world, I started each graph with what I consider the ideal. I know many churches that reach that ideal in each category. In fact, I have visited and investigated at least one church in each category that exceeds that "ideal"!

Responding (30 min.)

1. To begin responding to the local need for evangelism, read the statements from the bottom of page 141. Discuss ways in which the church should and could take action to change answers that the group feels are inadequate.
2. Discuss what the group thinks should be targets for their church, immediate and long range, in being a great commission church as found on the graph in handout 11c. Discuss briefly what first steps might be in reaching that goal.
3. Distribute graph on levels of involvement, "My Great Commission Investment" (handout 11d) and divide into quads. Spend 5-10 minutes in personal reflection and prayer and then put a "1" where you feel you are. If you feel the nudge of the Spirit that you need to make some changes and you have the faith to do it, tell God of your intention to take a step up and mark your target with a "2." One step will do! It's the direction that counts.

   If the groups have reached the level of intimacy needed for sharing the results of this self-evaluation, after a few minutes, suggest that they share with one another their present situation and their desires for the future. Follow up with a time of prayer for one another, person by person. If group sharing and prayer aren't appropriate, have a time of personal prayer.

Closure (5 min.)

1. Preview unit 12.
2. Offer a closing prayer of thanksgiving for the wonder that God would choose to do His work in this world through people like us. Pray for your church and those present that we may be all God wants us to be as true lovers of all the lost of the world.

After the Session

Review the prayer section in your spiritual journal and check each answer to prayer. Next time will be your last with the group. Make special prayer preparation for a great closing session.

If all your group is from your own church, do you have any results from today's activities that should be called to the attention of the church leadership? Might you take any other action to help your church maximize the youth's potential for great commission involvement?

A MARRIAGE MADE IN HEAVEN

Activity 10: Glorifying

The final time together should be a celebration of the freedom and joy of life in the Spirit. If circumstances permit, consider asking members to come early or to remain afterward for a "love feast," as it was called in New Testament times. Plan a meal or refreshments in whatever way fits your group. Let the meal be on the New Testament model of joyous fellowship with one another and the Lord—a small foretaste of the marriage banquet of the Bridegroom and the bride!

Session 12 Goals

Youth will:
- celebrate
- recall memory verses and activities of the Spirit
- relate the relationship of loving oneness with God to all the rest of the spiral.

Before the Session

❑ Refer to standard Before the Session procedures.
❑ Prepare the following items:
- a chart of the course outline with the memory verse Scripture reference for each unit
- a copy of the spiral for each member. Beside the spiral list the following: yield, trust, obey, know, love, companion, change, become like Jesus (handout 12a) (LG p. 61)
- a copy of the Christian Growth Study Plan (LG p. 63) for each member
- a hymnal for each member; or copies of the hymns and choruses you've used throughout the course.

During the Session

If you have a "love feast" before the session, bring it to a close before your final session.

Knowing (20 min.)

1. Recite each memory verse in unison.
2. Ask members to name the activities of the Spirit (found in day 5).

Understanding (25 min.)

1. Distribute copies of the spiral you have prepared, instructing them to discuss the order in which the terms *yield, trust, obey, know, love, companion, change, and become like Jesus* should appear on the spiral; that is, which response leads on to the next.

   Divide into quads and ask them to seek a consensus on the order of spiraling up, explaining that several legitimate possibilities exist.
2. Regather and ask for results from each quad, putting on the display chart what they say. Discuss the role of yield and trust until they are willing to put that at the beginning of the spiral up. Without that, nothing else can happen. Discuss the final goal until youth agree that loving oneness with God is what will happen when we see Him. Or, it is legitimate to put perfect likeness to Jesus at the top of the spiral.

   The main point of this exercise is to help youth feel the thrill of how these all interact and feed one another on each lap of the spiral: The more we know Him, the more we love Him; the more we love Him, the more we obey Him; the more we obey Him, the more like Him we become; the more like Him we become, the better we know Him; the more we know and love Him, the more we want to companion with Him; the more we companion with Him, the more we trust Him. On and on the spiral goes upward until we meet Jesus. And maybe after that as well! Wherever you start, after the initial turn-around—the unconditional yes of the soul (yield and trust)—the others follow, each making possible and, in turn, reinforcing the others.

Break (5 min.)

Experiencing and Responding (60 min.)

1. Have a time of testimony, inviting youth to share the greatest insight into life in the Spirit they have had through your 12 weeks together, or some experience that has greatly impacted their lives. You might suggest brief testimonies, with multiple opportunities to contribute rather than giving one long testimony.
2. Sing hymns of worship and love for God, celebrating our purpose in life to worship Him and declare His glories, expressing our deep desire of loving oneness with Him. If this catches on and many want to choose a hymn, you could ask them to choose one verse of the chosen hymn for all to sing.
3. Prayer time. Let each member express some praise, thanksgiving, or expression of love. Ask them not to make requests at this time, but to focus on worshiping God. Suggest they may want to quote from what they wrote in day 2.
4. Divide into quads and have a final time of prayer. Pray for each other specifically. Pray that the Spirit

will spiral each of you up into greater likeness to Jesus, more intimate companionship with our eternal lover. If the group has reached the level of openness to share personally, suggest that these prayers be specific for what they have learned is their friend's greatest desire or most difficult obstacle.

5. Closing hymn.

Closure (12 min.)

1. Hand out copies of the Christian Growth Study Plan form (LG p. 63) or ask youth to turn to page 160 and complete the Christian Growth Study Plan form in their books. Have them give you the forms as they leave the room.
2. Farewell and benediction.

After the Session

If you're particularly grateful for what God has done in answer to your prayers in this course, I'm sure He'd be glad to hear about it! Maybe it would be good to set aside a few minutes of quiet to review what has taken place in the lives of the people in your group (maybe checking out your prayer journal) and tell the Lord the specifics of your thanks.

Some special friendships may have developed, and you'll want to keep in touch with those. Be sure to pray for each member of your group for the first few weeks in order to conserve the fruit of your labor in leading them through this experience of life in the Spirit.

Mail the completed Christian Growth Study Plan forms to the address given on page 160 in the member book or page 63 in this Leader's Guide.

[KEEPING A SPIRITUAL JOURNAL]

Throughout this course you will have experiences in your spiritual life that you will want to record for later reference. When God speaks to you, you will want to write down what He says. You also will be given opportunity to pray specifically for members of your group and for your church. You will need a notebook of some kind. Assignments in the notebook will fall into four large categories. You may choose to create other categories if you want to.

Sections in your journal should include:

1. **Testimonies.** This section is for diary accounts of what God is doing in, around, and through your life and what you have learned about Him, His purposes, and His ways.

2. **Daily Review.** At the end of each day's work, you will be asked to review the lesson and identify the most meaningful statement or Scripture and then respond to God. The daily review section of your journal provides extra space for you to record summaries of what God is saying to you through His Word, prayer, circumstances, and the church. It also can include summaries of adjustments you sense God wants you to make, directions you sense God is calling you to follow, steps of obedience called for, and other responses God may be calling you to make to Him.

3. **Weekly Review.** Use the questions in the "Spiritual Journal Weekly Review" box at the right to review what God has done during the past week.

4. **Prayer Requests.** This section will be used in each group session for recording prayer requests and answers to prayer for individuals and for your church. It can be divided to include requests such as:
   - Personal requests
   - Requests for group members
   - Requests for my church
   - Other special requests

Spiritual Journal Weekly Review

Keeping a spiritual journal will help you remember the important things God says to you and the things He does in your life. Use the following questions to review God's activity in your life each week during this course of study. You only need to respond to those questions that apply to what God has done or revealed.

1. What has God revealed to you about Himself? (His name, His character, His nature)
2. What has God revealed to you about His purposes? (His will, His plans, His desires, His activity around you, His assignment to you, His goals, His objectives)
3. What has God revealed to you about His ways? (How He acts, what He does, how He responds in given circumstances, the kind of persons He uses, the ways He involves persons in His work, the ways He goes about accomplishing His purposes)
4. What has God done in your life or through your life that has caused you to experience His presence?
5. What Scripture has God used to speak to you about Himself, His purposes, or His ways?
6. What particular person or concern has God given you a burden to pray for? What has He guided you to pray for this person or concern?
7. What has God done through circumstances that has given you a sense of His timing or direction concerning any aspect of His will?
8. What word of guidance or truth do you sense God has spoken to you through another believer?
9. What adjustment is God leading you to make in your life?
10. What acts of obedience have you taken this week? What acts of obedience do you know God is wanting you to take?

Unit 1
We, who with unveiled faces all reflect the Lord's glory, are being transformed into his likeness with ever-increasing glory, which comes from the Lord, who is the Spirit.
–2 Corinthians 3:18, NIV

Unit 2
So God created human beings, making them to be like himself. He created them male and female.
–Genesis 1:27, GNB

Unit 3
All Scripture is inspired by God and is useful for teaching the truth, rebuking error, correcting faults, and giving instruction for right living, so that the person who serves God may be fully qualified and equipped to do every kind of good deed.
—2 Timothy 3:16-17, GNB

Unit 4
If anyone is in Christ, he is a new creation; the old has gone, the new has come!
—2 Corinthians 5:17, NIV

Unit 5
Do you not know that your body is the temple of the Holy Spirit, who is in you, whom you have received from God? You are not your own.
—1 Corinthians 6:19, NIV

The just shall live by his faith.
—Habakkuk 2:4, KJV

Unit 6
For this very reason, make every effort to add to your faith goodness; and to goodness, knowledge; and to knowledge, self-control; and to self-control, perseverance; and to perseverance, godliness; and to godliness, brotherly kindness; and to brotherly kindness, love. For if you possess these qualities in increasing measure, they will keep you from being ineffective and unproductive in your knowledge of our Lord Jesus Christ.
—2 Peter 1:5-8, NIV

Unit 7
Thanks be to God! He gives us the victory through our Lord Jesus Christ.
—1 Corinthians 15:57, NIV

Unit 8
Do not get drunk on wine, which leads to debauchery. Instead, be filled with the Spirit.
—Ephesians 5:18, NIV

The fruit of the Spirit is love, joy, peace, patience, kindness, goodness, faithfulness, gentleness and self-control.
—Galatians 5:22-23, NIV

Unit 9
Therefore, I urge you, brothers in view of God's mercy, to offer your bodies as living sacrifices, holy and pleasing to God—this is your spiritual act of worship. Do not conform any longer to the pattern of this world, but be transformed by the renewing of your mind. Then you will be able to test and approve what God's will is—his good, pleasing and perfect will.
–Romans 12:1-2, NIV

Unit 10
To each one the manifestation of the Spirit is given for the common good.
—1 Corinthians 12:7, NIV

Eagerly desire the greater gifts.
–1 Corinthians 12:31, NIV

Unit 11
"You will receive power when the Holy Spirit comes on you; and you will be my witnesses in Jerusalem, and in all Judea and Samaria, and to the ends of the earth."
—Acts 1:8, NIV

Unit 12
"I pray … that all of them may be one, Father, just as you are in me and I am in you. May they also be in us so that the world may believe that you have sent me.…I in them and you in me. May they be brought to complete unity to let the world know that you sent me and have loved them even as you have loved me."
—John 17:21,23, NIV

If the Spirit of him who raised Jesus from the dead is living in you, he who raised Christ from the dead will also give life to your mortal bodies through his Spirit, who lives in you.
—Romans 8:11, NIV

LEADER EVALUATION FORM

1. Did I appear to be adequately prepared? Why or why not?

____

2. What are specific areas needing more preparation? _______________________

____

3. Following our group session I felt we had reached our objectives:

	Very well									Hardly at all
Knowledge	10	9	8	7	6	5	4	3	2	1
Understanding	10	9	8	7	6	5	4	3	2	1
Experiencing	10	9	8	7	6	5	4	3	2	1
Responding	10	9	8	7	6	5	4	3	2	1

4. Our quad seems to be coming together in open communication. ❑ Yes ❑ No

5. Did I talk:
   - ❑ too much?
   - ❑ not enough—providing too little direction?

6. Was I sensitive to the concerns of members? ❑ Yes ❑ No

7. Was I successful in getting everyone to participate? ❑ Yes ❑ No

8. Was I enthusiastic about how God will use *Life in the Spirit* in member's lives and in our church? ❑ Yes ❑ No

9. What was the best thing about today's group session? _______________________

____

10. What part(s) of today's session needs improvement? _______________________

____

11. Suggestions on how to make that improvement. _______________________

____

12. Any other suggestions, comments, praises, concerns, you would like to express: ____________

____

____

LIFE in the SPIRIT
YOUTH EDITION

Do you want to ...

- Learn what the Holy Spirit is doing in the world today?
- Discover how you can live a Spirit-filled life?
- Experience life in a love relationship with the Spirit of God?

Life in the Spirit, will lead you in a 12-unit study of the Bible to learn how the Holy Spirit affects your life. Learn to see the Holy Spirit at work in Scripture and in your life. Examine how the Spirit designed you with a special purpose. Watch as the Spirit reveals God to the world and to you. Let the Spirit lead you up a spiral of growth to greater likeness to Jesus.

Interested?
Attend the introductory session:

DATE ______________________________

TIME ______________________________

PLACE ____________________________

Life in the Spirit

ATTENDANCE FORM

Date ____________

Name	Address	Phone	Paid/Date
			/
			/
			/
			/
			/
			/
			/
			/
			/
			/
			/
			/
			/
			/
			/
			/

You have permission to reproduce this page for use with your *Life in the Spirit* group.

STANDARD BEFORE THE SESSION

Cut on the dotted line and use these standard checklists before and after each group session. You might want to laminate these cut-out sections and use as a bookmark for this guide.

BEFORE THE SESSION

The following suggestions for preparation are standard for each of the 12 small-group sessions. They will be referenced but not repeated.

1. Complete all the learning activities for the current unit in the member's book.
2. Pause and pray for God's guidance as you prepare for this week's group session. Pray for each member of your group.
3. Secure the hymns or choruses you choose.
4. Read through "During the Session." Decide on the amount of time to allow for each activity and write the time in the margin you think each activity should begin. Always be prepared to change your plans if the Holy Spirit should lead you and the group in another direction.
5. Prepare a two-minute overview of the next unit.
6. Secure pencils, paper, or other needed supplies.

AFTER THE SESSION

The following suggestions for preparation are standard for each of the 12 small-group sessions. They will be referenced but not repeated.

1. Record in the prayer section of your own spiritual journal specific ways you can pray for group members. Do you sense a need to pray intently for any one youth in particular? If so, record concerns you need to pray about for that person.

2. Ask yourself the following questions and make notes in your journal.
   - What resources, if any, do I need to get for group members? Does everyone have a member's book and spiritual journal?
   - What spiritual or mental preparation do I need to make for the next session that may have been lacking this week?
   - Which members need to be encouraged to participate more in the sharing and discussion times? When and how will I encourage them?
   - When could I have responded more appropriately to the needs of the youth or to the leadership of the Holy Spirit?
   - How well did I do at beginning and ending on time?
   - Which youth most need a phone call this week for encouragement, prayer, instruction, correction, or counsel? When shall I make the calls?

3. Read through "Before the Session" for the next session to get an idea of the preparation that will be required for your next group session.

GET ACQUAINTED

a. Name ______________________________

b. Address ______________________________

c. Phone ______________

d. What I like best about my home town …

____

____

e. I accepted Jesus Christ as my Lord and Savior when…

____

____

f. Something interesting you might not know about me …

____

____

____

g. I chose to study this course on *Life in the Spirit* because…

____

____

____

UNIT 1 REVIEW QUIZ

1. What is God's standard for Christian living? ____

____

2. What is God's provision for the Christian to meet that standard? Unscramble the letters for the two answers.

A WNE NIRACTOE   A WNE ROSETILPHANI

• _ ___ ________   • _ ___ ____________

3. What is my responsibility for using God's provision? Fill in the blanks. (See day 3.)

• K___

• S________

• T____

4. What results can I expect in my personal life if I fulfill that responsibility? Complete the following sentences. (See p. 17)

1. We become ____

2. We get ____

3. We get ____

5. What does God expect of me in reaching out to others? Give at least two answers.

UNIT 2 REVIEW QUIZ

1. Although a "spiritual" person might be all the following, check the most comprehensive.
   - ❑ having a spirit as well as a body
   - ❑ interested in the unseen
   - ❑ Christlike in behavior
   - ❑ religious
   - ❑ experiences life in the Spirit
   - ❑ sensitive to the needs of others

2. Underline the characteristic in each pair that best describes the Holy Spirit.

a. personal	impersonal
b. a name for God	one person of the godhead
c. created before time	uncreated
d everywhere present	sent on special tasks
e. comes when a believer calls	is always present in every believer

3. Check everything in the following list that is part of our likeness to God.
   - ❑ ability to think
   - ❑ capacity to love God and be loved of Him
   - ❑ ability to talk
   - ❑ conscience: knowing moral right from wrong
   - ❑ body
   - ❑ God-compatible spirit
   - ❑ creative

Put an asterisk (*) beside the answer you like best or are most grateful for.

4. What is the ultimate reason God made you like Himself? ______________________________

____

5. Check those items which you expect God to accomplish in you in your lifetime:
   - ❑ 1. daily sense of companionship with God
   - ❑ 2. unfailing Christlike behavior
   - ❑ 3. consistent victory over my temptations
   - ❑ 4. steady growth toward likeness to Jesus
   - ❑ 5. attitudes of perfect love, joy, peace, patience, purity, contentment, and humility

Put an asterisk (*) beside the answer you feel He has best accomplished in you already.

UNIT 3 REVIEW QUIZ

Put a *T* by all that are wholly true and *F* by any that are wholly or partly false.

1.___ In the Bible the Holy Spirit revealed all the truth worth knowing.

2.___ Inspiration means that the Holy Spirit dictated to the human authors of Scripture the very words He wanted to communicate.

3.___ The authority of a statement for the hearer or reader depends on who said it.

4.___ The purpose of interpretation is to find the meaning intended by the author.

5.___ All interpretations are equally valid.

6.___ *Illumination* is the term used to indicate the way the Spirit inspired Bible authors.

7.___ Since the Bible is a supernatural book, the interpreter should look for hidden, spiritual meanings in each passage, especially when seeking guidance.

8.___ Bible believing Christians can't agree on more than about 50 percent of what the Bible text means.

9.___ One true interpretation always exists, but there may be many true applications of a Bible teaching.

10.___ We're pretty much on our own when it comes to understanding and applying the Bible.

11.___ Those who point out error in Scripture are actually putting their judgment over biblical authority.

12.___ I should treat Scripture as infallible, but not my every interpretation of it.

13.___ Only those who intend to obey a Bible teaching can be confident of their understanding of it.

14.___ We studied seven distinct ways in which the Bible reveals God's will for my life.

15.___ Some people use the term *interpretation* to indicate a meaning imposed on the plain statement of Scripture, even if it's unrelated to the author's intended meaning.

Handout 3b

Name one interpretation of Scripture you have heard that bothers you most. Circle which of the following is the chief problem.

a. Understanding the author's meaning

b. Difficulty in obeying the clear teaching

c. Confidence that the passage is really from God

d. The interpreter has used a naturalistic approach, treating the Bible as a purely human effort

e. The interpreter has used a supernaturalistic (magical) or intuitive approach

f. The interpreter has imposed a meaning on the text from her or his own tradition, cultural background, or personal preference

UNIT 4 REVIEW QUIZ

1. In this unit we focused more on Jesus than on the Holy Spirit, so it may surprise you to realize we considered at least 8 activities of the Spirit! In the short blanks, name as many of the activities as possible.

__________ ______________________________

__________ ______________________________

__________ ______________________________

__________ ______________________________

__________ ______________________________

__________ ______________________________

__________ ______________________________

__________ ______________________________

2. Now in the margin to the left of each activity, number them in the order they must be experienced. In other words, without the preceding activity, the Spirit can't accomplish the next. Hint: this is not the same order we studied them in the unit.

3. Now, in the line following each activity, explain why you put it in the order you did. For example, it's clear that I couldn't be born again if Jesus hadn't died, so "regeneration" can't come before His sacrificial death to provide for my salvation.

a. For Christ to be in me means ...

b. For me to be in Christ means ...

c. What I like about the law is ...

d. What I don't like about the law is ...

Unit 6 Review Quiz

1. What is the first step in the path of spiraling upward toward likeness to Jesus and oneness with God?

2. What are at least three major means of grace ("tools of the Spirit") that help us grow as we participate with the Spirit?

3. Why do some Christians fail to grow spiritually? Name three potential blocks to spiraling up.

4. In unit 6 I told two stories of spiraling up, Matusyama's and my own. What is your story? Write it out briefly below.

UNIT 6 CONCEPT CHECKUP

1. True-False. Be careful to mark *F* if any part of the statement is incorrect.

_____ a. All Christians are growing, it's just that some grow faster than others.

_____ b. No Christian ever need repent—that was done once for all at conversion.

_____ c. Growth begins with surrender to the will of God and continues from then on whether a person is intentional about it or not.

_____ d. A person can grow in quality of Christian character, but you can't grow in surrender or faith—you either have them or not.

_____ e. The ultimate goal of our upward spiral is Christlike behavior.

2. What one response is always needed to change adverse circumstances into blessings? ____________________

____

____

3. Suffering may come from many sources. Mark through any that are never the source of suffering.

- The devil
- God
- Sin—my own or someone else's
- The natural result of living in a fallen world
- Other people: enemies, friends, strangers
- Error or mistake—my own or someone else's

4. Circle each of the following that are never God's purposes in allowing you to suffer.

- To bring Him glory
- Discipline resulting from sin
- Growth toward Christlikeness
- Guidance—leading us to do something we might not otherwise do
- To make us miserable so we'll want to go to heaven
- Testing our faith

UNIT 7 REVIEW QUIZ

1. Name 6 or 7 activities of the Holy Spirit studied thus far.

2. As completely as possible, state a biblical definition of *sin.* Incorporate the concepts we studied in day 3.

3. In day 4 we distinguished two kinds of victory we can expect, depending on the variety of sin we are thinking about (1. deliberate or willful, 2. unintentional, 3. resulting from slavery). What are they?

BIBLICAL BALANCE IN THE CHRISTIAN LIFE

Handout 7b

1. God's standard: that we become like Jesus

Beside each example write either an *L* for too low or *H* for too high an expectation of success. Then write your own statement of what you can expect with regard to becoming like Christ.

___ a. Cheryl has achieved absolute perfection.
___ b. Don expects to be less than a conqueror.
___ c. Allison settles for a defeated pattern of life.
___ d. John hasn't sinned in five years.

My statement: Regarding becoming like Jesus, I ______________________________

____

____

2. God's provision: the Holy Spirit

Beside each example write either *SE* for self-effort or *NE* for no effort (avoiding responsibility by expecting the Spirit to do it all). Then write your own statement of the Holy Spirit's role in Christlike living.

___ a. It all depends on me.
___ b. Let go and let God.
___ c. Spectator Christianity: get out of the way and let God do everything.
___ d. God helps those who help themselves.

My statement: The Holy Spirit's role is ______________________________

____

____

3. My responsibility: obedient faith

Beside each example write either *F* for feels powerless to do anything about it or *T* for take it for granted. Then write your own statement of your duty to respond in faith.

___ a. "Name-it-and-claim-it" faith
___ b. Whatever will be will be
___ c. If you only have faith, you'll be healthy and have abundance always
___ d. Sin is inevitable

My statement: My responsibility for faith means ______________________________

____

____

Handout 8a

UNIT 8 REVIEW QUIZ

1. List three biblical meanings of the picture words, *filled with the Spirit.*

1.

2.

3.

2. After each meaning note a date, a time in your life, or an occasion on which you feel you experienced the Spirit's filling in that sense.

Handout 8b

UNIT 8 TRUE OR FALSE QUIZ

Mark *T* for every statement that is wholly true and *F* for every statement that is wholly or partly false.

____ 1. I'm the best one to judge whether I'm filled with the Spirit based on spiritual fruit.

____ 2. The word *revival* actually refers to the experience of a group of Christians rather than to unbelievers or an individual Christian.

____ 3. You can experience a personal revival whether or not others participate.

____ 4. A person who is already full of the Holy Spirit can be "filled."

____ 5. When it comes to an inner feeling of fullness only others can judge whether I'm truly full.

____ 6. Being full of the Spirit refers first of all to a relationship between two persons.

____ 7. This is the first unit in which we've studied the fruit of the Spirit.

UNIT 8 PRAYER GUIDE

1. Private prayer. Reaffirm your relationship to the Holy Spirit as unconditional Lord of life with no fine print in the contract, no conditions. If you have never made such a commitment, consider doing so now.

2. Share with the group the fruit you're asking the Spirit to give you more of (p.105, mb). You can explain your desire briefly if you feel it would help. After each person shares, the person to his or her right should pray, asking God to give a bumper crop of that fruit.

3. Share with the group any hope you may have for greater power in some ministry you have or you are contemplating. After sharing, the person to the left should pray for the Spirit to grant that request.

4. Prayer time for revival in your local church.

5. Prayer time for revival in the whole church in the United States and worldwide.

Handout 10a

Purposes of the church	*Gifts that contribute to that purpose*
Worship	______________________________
Fellowship	______________________________
Discipleship	______________________________
Ministry	______________________________
Evangelism	______________________________

Handout 10b

Lord, speak to me, that I may speak
In living echoes of thy tone;
As thou hast sought, so let me seek
Thy erring children lost and lone.

O teach me, Lord, that I may teach
The precious things thou dost impart;
And wing my words, that they may reach
The hidden depths of many a heart.

O fill me with thy fullness, Lord,
Until my very heart o'er flow
In kindling tho't and glowing word,
Thy love to tell, thy praise to show.

O use me, Lord, use even me,
Just as thou wilt, and when and where;
Until thy blessed face I see,
Thy rest, thy joy, thy glory share.

—Frances R. Havergal

THE PROGRESS OF WORLD EVANGELISM

The long quotation below is from the Manila Manifesto, edited by John R. Stott at the global Lausanne Congress in Manila, in July of 1989.

The Challenge of AD 2000 and Beyond

The world population is approaching 6 billion. One third nominally confess Christ. Of the remaining 4 billion, half have heard of Him, half have not. In the light of these figures, we evaluate our evangelistic task by considering 4 categories of people.

First, **the committed** constitute the potential missionary work force. In this century this category of Christian believers has grown from about 40 million in 1900 to about 500 million in 1989, and at this moment is growing over twice as fast as any other major religious group.

Secondly, **the uncommitted** make a Christian profession (they have been baptized, attend church occasionally and even call themselves Christians), but the notion of a personal commitment to Christ is foreign to them. They are found in all churches throughout the world. They urgently need to be re-evangelized.

Thirdly, **the unevangelized** are people who have a minimal knowledge of the gospel but have had no valid opportunity to respond to it. They are probably within reach of Christian people if only these will go to the next street, road, village or town to find them.

Fourthly, **the unreached** are 2 billion people who may never have heard of Jesus as Savior, and are not within reach of Christians of their own people. Some 2,000 peoples or nationalities do not yet have a vital, indigenous church movement. We find it helpful to think of them as belonging to smaller 'people groups' that perceive themselves as having an affinity with each other (e.g. a common culture, language, home, or occupation). The most effective messengers to reach them will (would) be those believers who already belong to their culture and know their language. Otherwise, missionaries must go, leaving behind their own culture and sacrificially identifying with the people they long to reach for Christ.

About 11,000 such unreached people groups exist within the 2,000 larger peoples, so that the task is not impossible. Yet at the present only 7% of all missionaries are engaged in this kind of outreach, while the remaining 93% are working in the already evangelized half of the world. If this imbalance is to be redressed, a strategic redeployment of personnel will be necessary...

We are deeply ashamed that nearly two millennia have passed since the death and resurrection of Jesus, and two-thirds of the world's population have not yet acknowledged Him. On the other hand, we are amazed at the mounting evidence of God's power even in the most unlikely places of the globe. Christ commands us to take the gospel to all peoples. The task is urgent. We are determined to obey him with joy and hope. (John R. Stott, Manila Manifesto)

For every Bible-believing Christian in the world only four people (Group D) are still behind cultural and linguistic barriers sealed off from any normal gospel witness. Never before have we been so close to the end of the remaining specifically *missionary* task.

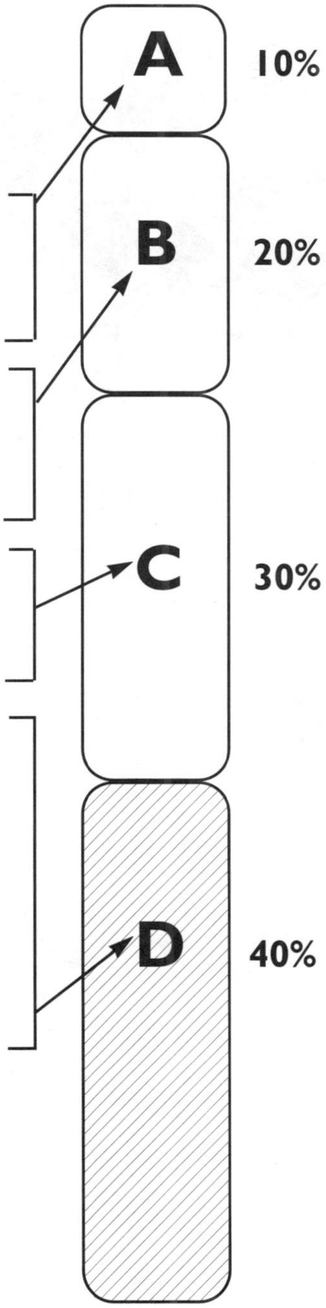

1 out of 10 of the world's population = 570 million Bible-believing Christians who are the potential work force in missions.

2 out of 10 of the world's population = 1,300 million other Christians who need to be "renewed or re-evangelized to help [The slowest growing block of humanity—dragging down the "average growth rate" of all Christians]*

3 out of 10 of the world's population = 1,660 million non-Christians already within reach of Christian people—these are within "reached groups," needing ordinary evangelism not missions.

4 out of 10 of the world's population = 2,170 million non-Christians outside the reach of Christians of their own people—these live within "Unreached groups"—e.g. there is no viable, indigenous, evangelizing church movement within their "nation, people, tribe or tongue." They need the special kind of evangelism called "missions."

Summary:
1 = 570 (A)
2 = 1,300 (B)
3 = 1,660 (C)
4 = 2,170 (D)
10 = 5,700
(= world population, roughly mid 1994)

*Note: 90% of the world's missionaries work with groups B and C, where missionary work has already had great success. This leaves only 10% to push on into the final domain of group D.

The 55 Least Evangelized Countries & the 10/40 Window

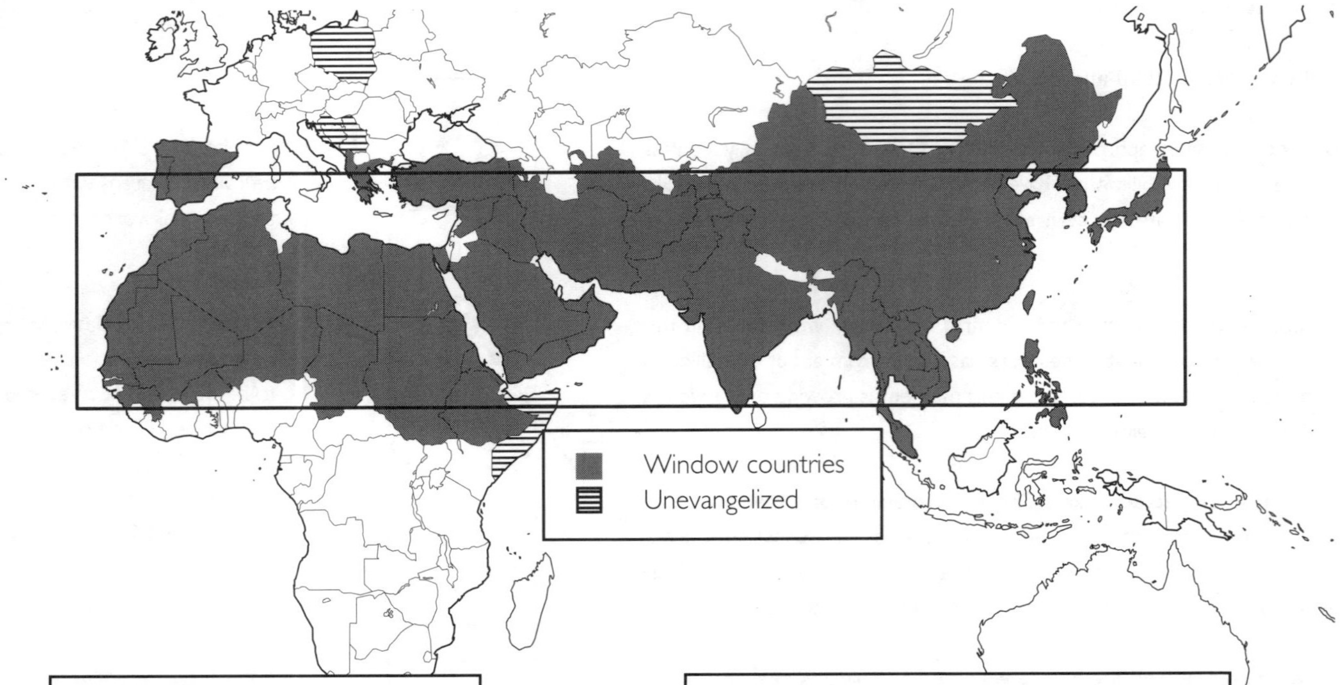

INSIDE THE WINDOW
62 Countries
Total Population 3.1 Billion
60% of the World's Population
27% of the Missionaries
22% Muslim, 23% Hindu,
5% Buddhist

LEAST EVANGELIZED COUNTRIES
55 Countries
Total Population 3.0 Billion
57% of the World's Population
18% of the Missionaries
23% Muslim, 24% Hindu,
4% Buddhist

Handout 11c

GREAT COMMISSION CHURCH PROFILE

Local witness and evangelism: percent of our church membership who were baptized as new believers last year:

5%	3%	2%	0%

Amount of time our church spends in prayer each week in groups of people or as a congregation for missionaries and/or the unreached people of the world:

1 hour	15 minutes	5 minutes	0 minutes

Percent of our total membership who have gone into pioneer mission work as a vocation:

10%	5%	2%	0%

Percent of our total church income that is invested in missions outside the local church area:

50%	30%	20%	10%	0%

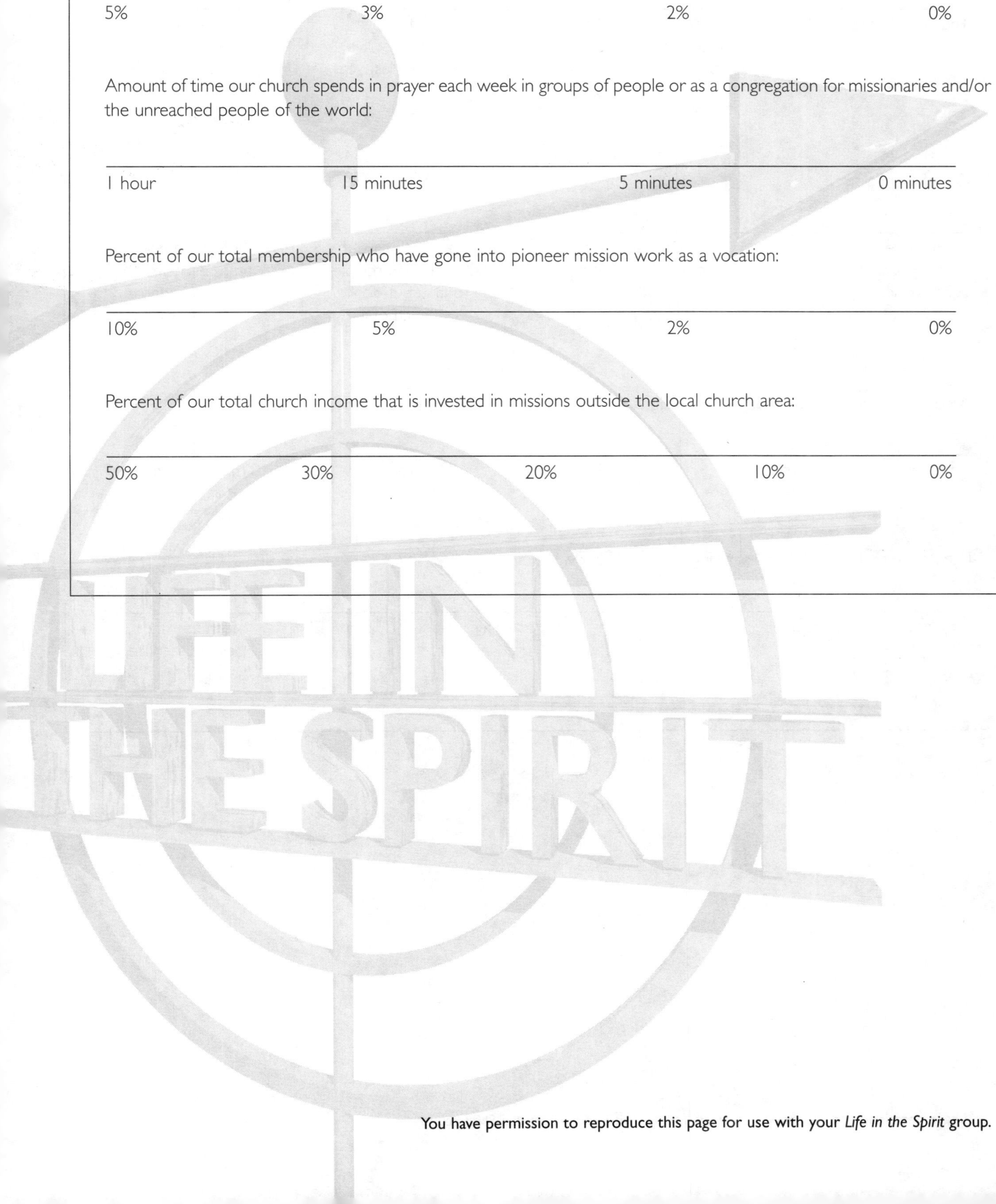

Handout 11d

MY GREAT COMMISSION INVESTMENT

My level of faithfulness in witness:

The past year I shared my faith with no one	When others initiated the conversation, I talked about my faith	I shared my faith with at least five unbelievers last year	I regularly talk about spiritual things with friends, coworkers, and those I meet.

Gift of evangelism:

I don't have the gift of evangelism, and don't particularly want it.	I don't have the gift of evangelism but pray God will give it to me.	I think I may have the ability to win people to faith but don't do much of it.	At least several times each year I win someone to Christ.

Amount of time I spend in prayer for missionaries and/or some unreached group of people:

never	occasionally	weekly	5 minutes daily	10 minutes or more

During the past year my level of giving to God's work was:

very little	impulse	tithe	manager	sacrificial	faith for funds beyond sacrifice

Handout 12a

SPIRALING UP

Beside the spiral below write the following in the order they occur as we live life in the Spirit:
know, companion, yield, change, become like Jesus, trust, love, obey.

[LIFE IN THE SPIRIT GROUP COVENANT]

I,________________________________covenant with my Life in the Spirit group to do the following.

1. Complete the study of *Life in the Spirit* workbook each week before the group session.

2. Pray regularly for the other group members.

3. Participate in all group sessions. (If unable to attend due to circumstance beyond my control, I'll make up the session at the earliest possible time.)

4. Participate openly and honestly in the group sessions.

5. Keep confidential any personal matters shared by others in the group.

6. Be patient with my Christian brothers and sisters and my church as God works to make us what He wants us to be. I'll trust God to convince others of His will. I will not try to manipulate or pressure others to do what I think is best.

7. Others:

Signed:____Date:________________

Life in the Spirit Group Members:

____________________________ ____________________________

____________________________ ____________________________

____________________________ ____________________________

____________________________ ____________________________

____________________________ ____________________________

CHRISTIAN GROWTH STUDY PLAN

Preparing Christians to Serve

In the **Christian Growth Study Plan (formerly Church Study Course),** this book *Life in the Spirit, Youth Edition* is a resource for course credit in the subject area "Personal Life" of the Christian Growth category of diploma plans. To receive credit, read the book, complete the learning activities, show your work to your pastor, a staff member or church leader, then complete the following information. This page may be duplicated. Send the completed page to:

Christian Growth Study Plan
127 Ninth Avenue, North, MSN 117
Nashville, TN 37234-0117
FAX: (615)251-5067

For information about the Christian Growth Study Plan, refer to the current Christian Growth Study Plan Catalog. Your church office may have a copy. If not, request a free copy from the Christian Growth Study Plan office (615/251-2525).

Life in the Spirit, Youth Edition

COURSE NUMBER: CG-0379

PARTICIPANT INFORMATION

Social Security Number (USA ONLY)	Personal CGSP Number*	Date of Birth (MONTH, DAY, YEAR)
- -	- -	- -

Name (First, Middle, Last)	Home Phone
☐ Mr. ☐ Miss ☐ Mrs. ☐	- -

Address (Street, Route, or P.O. Box)	City, State, or Province	Zip/Postal Code

CHURCH INFORMATION

Church Name		
Address (Street, Route, or P.O. Box)	City, State, or Province	Zip/Postal Code

CHANGE REQUEST ONLY

☐ Former Name		
☐ Former Address	City, State, or Province	Zip/Postal Code
☐ Former Church	City, State, or Province	Zip/Postal Code

Signature of Pastor, Conference Leader, or Other Church Leader	Date

*New participants are requested but not required to give SS# and date of birth. Existing participants, please give CGSP# when using SS# for the first time. Thereafter, only one ID# is required. **Mail to:** Christian Growth Study Plan, 127 Ninth Ave., North, Nashville, TN 37234-0117. Fax: (615)251-5067

[EXTRAS]

Attention Youth and Youth Leaders! If you enjoyed this study on Life in the Spirit, check out these other books! They are available at your LifeWay Christian Book Store, the Baptist Book Store, or by calling Toll-free 1-800-458-2772.

Lift High the Torch: An Invitation to Experiencing God

by Henry Blackaby

Lay the ground work for your Experiencing God study with this introductory book—a four-part call to holiness using brief chapters and lots of think-through activities. It's an ideal way to get hearts right and attitudes adjusted, preparing your teenagers for the experience of their lives! (4 sessions)

08054 9847 8 • $2.95

In God's Presence, Youth Edition

by T.W. Hunt and Claude V. King

Designed to encourage youth to develop a strong prayer life that is active and exciting, this six-week prayer exercise will expose youth to the elements of prayer in a positive way.

They'll learn to use the power of prayer to experience God through confession, petition, worship, praise, thanksgiving, and intercession. Learning activities for leading a group session are included as well.

07673 0001 7 • $6.95

Experiencing God: Knowing and Doing the Will of God, Youth Edition

by Henry Blackaby and Claude King

Lead youth in this exciting, truly compelling 9-week study of the Bible and help them learn to hear when God is speaking; find out where God is working and join Him; and experience God doing what only He can do.

Member's Book 08054 9925 3 • $9.95
Leader's Guide 08054 9924 5 • $6.95

Experiencing God Youth Video Series

A set of two videos. Henry Blackaby leads you through the first one, answering most commonly asked questions about the course. The second video is Blackaby and youth interacting in a fast-paced give-and-take video complete with discussion starters for use during your weekly study group.

Video Series 08054 9839 7 • $49.95

The Mind of Christ, Youth Edition

by T.W. Hunt and Claude V. King

Help your youth put on the Mind of Christ as found in Philippians 2:5-11 with this 12 unit daily study book. With it, they'll come to understand more

of what Christ desires of them, while they're challenged to explore the truths of experiencing freedom in Christ, the virtues of Godly wisdom, the art of servanthood, living in the Spirit, and exalting Christ.

Member's Book 07673 0009 • $10.95
Facilitator's Guide 07673 2585 0 • $5.95